2,50

Essay Index

TWENTIETH CENTURY
FRENCH WRITERS

Frontispiece

Mary Duclaux

TWENTIETH CENTURY
FRENCH WRITERS

(REVIEWS AND REMINISCENCES)

BY

MADAME MARY DUCLAUX

Essay Index

Essay Index Reprint Series

BOOKS FOR LIBRARIES PRESS
FREEPORT, NEW YORK

First Published 1920
Reprinted in this Series 1966, 1969

STANDARD BOOK NUMBER:
8369-1330-2

LIBRARY OF CONGRESS CATALOG CARD NUMBER:
67-22089

PRINTED IN THE UNITED STATES OF AMERICA

PRE-WAR PREFACE

I MEANT this book to be an image, a reflection, of the Twentieth Century in France, so far as it is shown in literature during the first fourteen years of its course. But my book is small, the subject is vast : an actual, living movement, a growing generation, is a difficult thing to copy—it will not keep still ! And it branches out so wide : there are so many French writers of the younger sort ! I am overcome with remorse when I think of the gifted beings whom I have left out !

I remember that child whom Saint Augustine saw, trying to gather the sea into his little shell; like him, I see the waters stretching illimitably : I have only brought away a sample. Yet those who taste it may have some faint idea, if not of the breadth and the numerousness of the literary movement in France, at least of its savour and its quality.

Given the limits of my little volume, I was compelled to make a choice; and there is always some injustice in a selection. Why should some be taken and others left? Why accept Rostand and reject Bataille? Why give Madame de Noailles and say nothing of Fernand Gregh? Why gather up Boylesve and André Gide, neglecting Estaunie, and Sageret, and Paul Adam? If I have Marie Lenéru, why not Sacha Guitry? Choosing Madame

PRE-WAR PREFACE

Colette, what reason have I for eliminating Madame de Régnier or Madame Delarue-Mardrus? I especially mourn the absence of the Brothers Tharaud, those perfect artists, who preserve the tradition of Flaubert. And there is a great gap in my fabric where I should have put the colonial novel (that flourishing Euphorion, born of the union of Loti and Kipling). Why have I not a line for Henry Daguerches, for Claude Farrère? All these are names to remember.

At least I lay this unction to my soul: if I have not always chosen the most perfect, I have faithfully gone in for the most characteristic.

Having to choose a remnant, I have taken those who, instead of continuing the traditions of the Nineteenth Century, have said a new thing, boldly differing, starting forth on a fresh career of their own. I have 'plumped' for the daring apostles of Life, those who cultivate movement and liberty rather than Art; freedom of rhythm rather than classic determinism and classic constraint; all those whose method tends to the condition of music, who say with the Abbess Hildegard (and with Bergson), 'Symphonialis est anima.' Such authors as these are emphatically of the youth of the world, and the most difficult for a foreign public to distinguish.

My readers will probably find most of these names new; they may even be disappointed at not meeting with those more illustrious spirits with whom for five-and-twenty years they have

PRE-WAR PREFACE

been familiar : Pierre Loti, Paul Bourget, Anatole France. These great writers still shed on the Twentieth Century the lustre its predecessor brought them; but they are the glorious past, and our concern is with the future. These younger men are the French equivalents to our Wells, and Galsworthy, and Hewlett, our Granville, Barker, our Synge, and Yeats, our Masefield and our Joseph Conrad, nay, even our Compton Mackenzie and our Lascelles Abercrombie. And my task is rendered more difficult by the fact that France is a twy-creature, of double nature, a sort of two-headed eagle or Rosa-Josepha among nations.

There is, I believe, one of the South American republics which possesses a couple of capitals : one to be used when the Liberals are in power, and one for the Conservatives. France also has a double set of everything, including celebrities : those admired by the *bien-pensant*, and those peculiar to the *intellectuels*. You may be illustrious in one group and barely heard of in the other. Those who adore Anatole France and praise Romain Rolland smile sarcastic at the name of Barrès, and have never opened a book by Paul Claudel. And, of course, it is the same the other way round—only more so.

I have done my best to hold the balance even : to group on the Right my seemly sheep, and on the Left my free-ranging goats, in flocks of approximate number, setting Boylesve over against Jules Renard, and Francis Jammes in front of Charles-Louis Philippe. If my reader discover that which all have in common, I think he may have a fair idea of the trend and the thrust of the spirit of the age—at least, so far as it is manifest in fiction, in poetry, and in the more literary drama, that 'spectacle dans un fauteuil' which may or may not be a spectacle for the stage.

What I have not shown him—to my real regret, to my recurrent remorse—is the world of the critics, the intellectual flower of France. I am not speaking of the reviewers; but of critics in the sense that Carlyle, Matthew Arnold, Taine, Renan were critics—the moralists, the biographers, the portrait-painters of a soul, an epoch, or a race. In France what branch of literature is more important than such criticism? Who has more charm than Suarès, with his imaginative and morbid studies of great souls? Who forms the mind of a generation more plastically than the brilliant and perspicacious André Chevrillon? Who interprets human nature more intimately than André Gide, or the acute and icy Julien Benda, or the romantic and religious Fortunat Strowski, the historian of Pascal; or the humane and sensitive Daniel Halévy, with his passionate Nietzsche, his strong and suffering Proudhon? These, perhaps, occupy less space in the booksellers' windows than our novelists and poets, but they are factors as considerable in the education of a race. I salute them, even as, perforce, I pass them by. Perhaps another year I may reserve another book for them.

MARY DUCLAUX.

AFTERWORDS—AFTERWARDS

In August, 1914, this little book was already in the printer's hands, the last revise corrected, the 'paste-up' prepared, ready to appear in the autumn, when certain events, which we all remember, happened with the suddenness of a thunderclap. The season was not favourable to the production of books, and for nearly five years neither author nor publisher gave the volume a thought. The Twentieth Century writer was elbowed out of the field by the Twentieth Century fighter. Alas, too often the one has been buried in the grave of the other, and the young man of letters whose fame and fortune we were announcing has fallen into nameless dust, or lies hidden under one of these innumerable slim gray crosses that spring, like some strange new harvest, on the low hills round Verdun, or along the valleys of the Marne and the Somme.

When, in the Spring of 1919, Messrs Collins returned me my old revise for a last glance ere it finally went to press, I gazed in consternation at the pages which had seemed so reasonable five years ago. Five years? Let us say ten years! 'Les années de campagne comptent double.' It was like opening an old bundle of photographs after a great lapse of time—the same mixture of melancholy, and a sort of sad amusement. Look at this absurd youth! Who could have supposed that he would become so famous? And that brilliant creature, dead now, and already half-forgotten. So-and-so, at least, has developed along the lines that we laid down and has turned out just the successful and useful servant of civilisation that we imagined.

In our case, So-and-so is Barrès. He has become all that we thought he might become. Public life and the patriotic duty have absorbed him more and more; he has been to the France of 1914-19 something of that which Lamartine was in 1848. He, more than any, has preached the need of union—'L'Union sacrée,' bringing into public affairs a largeness of outlook and sweetness of temper rare in politics,—especially in France. Few of these eloquent pages which day by day he has contributed to the *Echo de Paris* will remain as works of literature, but, piled up, no longer read, in their accumulation they form a pedestal which certainly heightens the moral importance of the man. Here at least we have the satisfaction of finding our analysis exact. More and more, in these days of storm and stress, Barrès has 'felt the need of merging himself in something larger and more durable than any individual existence'; 'no longer the singular, the extraordinary attracts him;' he finds something pleasant and satisfying in the alliance of courage and the spirit of adventure, 'with a certain soldierly mediocrity of mind'

AFTERWORDS—AFTERWARDS

—and all the more when their conjunction 'promises the conquest of Alsace-Lorraine.' Above all, he has given himself heart and soul to 'the creation of a truly National Party, capable of bringing out of chaos a new organic order.' Shall we not say of him that, like his heroine, Colette, 'Il se sent chargé d'une grande dignité, soulevé vers quelquechose de plus vaste, de plus haut, et de plus constant que sa personne'?

Yes, I can re-read the chapter on Barrès with a certain satisfaction.

But, when we come to Romain Rolland, what a falling-off was there! How is it that Romain Rolland, who seemed, if such there was, the very prophet and the teacher of the younger generation, should have proved so much less sure as a guide and a standby than the fantastic and singular Barrès? Always an aloof and solitary spirit, Rolland completely detached himself from his country during the war. In his voluntary exile at Geneva he occupied his hands, and no doubt his heart, with works of mercy, but his mind gave no support to his compatriots. Doubtless the attraction of Germany was too strong : 'Jean Christophe' continued to subjugate the delicate 'Oliver.' These great international friendships have their perils (and, doubtless, I speak of them in the mood of Bishop Berkeley : 'There, but for the Grace of God, go I !') Yet Renan was no less attached to intellectual Germany than Rolland : Renan, who, when his mind crossed the Rhine, 'crut entrer dans un temple,' and in 1870-71 France had no firmer patriot than Ernest Renan.

The fact is that Romain Rolland's genius is not French. The son of the lawyer at Clamecy is French enough by descent and as good a Burgundian as Lamartine, but he ought to have been Swiss by nature as by choice. There is nothing Latin or classic in him. His intense individualism, his moral earnestness, his lyric love of nature, and something querimonious, a scolding tenderness in his voice, remind us sometimes of Rousseau. And never was his high-minded crankiness more apparent than in that untimely pamphlet—'Au dessus de la Mêlée,' in which he rubbed it into us so tactlessly that our preoccupations are not his who dwells, unfriended, melancholy remote, above the fray.

This little volume made him probably the most unpopular writer in France. There is a radical misunderstanding which separates Romain Rolland from the young Frenchmen of the war. How has it come about? Hamlet and Harry Hotspur were good friends when we took leave of them in the final chapters of *Jean-Christophe*. Few men of letters had more vividly appreciated the active, ingenuous, hardy generation that was taking its first flights in the aeroplanes of 1912 and 1913. Arrogant, gay and strong, cheerful in their bright materialism (which allied itself so naturally with the most orthodox acquiescence in the creed of their forefathers), the tall and sturdy race of

AFTERWORDS—AFTERWARDS

the Twentieth Century pleased Jean-Christophe, because they seemed so prosperous and so happy —and that is, after all, what we chiefly ask of those who are to take our place in life.

M. Rolland liked these young men; still, he expected them to look up to him; he felt himself their moral and intellectual superior, as doubtless he was. But then the war broke out, and what a reversal of values! Most of us, in France, who sheltered behind the brave broad shoulders of our 'poilus,' felt our hearts melt with admiration, pity, hope, and love. Not so, M. Rolland.

His attitude has been one of irritable self-defence. First of all that pamphlet, 'Au dessus de la Mêlée'—and now this new book, published to-day (April, 1919), but finished (M. Rolland tells us) in May, 1914. *Colas Breugnon* is a study in Rabelais' vein. But, if M. Rolland's style is far from perfect when he writes as from the Twentieth Century, what an exasperating gallimaufry it becomes, what a pretentious farrago of lyrism, puns, blank-verse, conceits, and quips, when he assumes the character of one of his ancestors; a certain joiner and cabinet-maker at Clamecy, under the reign of Louis XIII. The rough jokes of the tavern chronicled in the style of Euphues! Romain Rolland maundering of Women, Wine, and Song! The worst of it is that his boozing and his babble do not seem genuine: the professor's gown peeps from under the starched blue folds of the carpenter's blouse. It is as though, irritated by the reproach of internationalism and cosmopolitanism, M. Rolland had said to himself, 'After all, I am neither a Jew nor a foreigner! If Péguy came from Orleans, I come from Clamecy; I have just as good French blood in my veins as he.' And behold him capering unconvincingly as a Burgundian artisan, drowning his troubles in the bowl.

I wonder if any of my readers remember a French country novel called *Le Moulin du Frau*, which appeared about 1894, by Eugène le Roy, the author of *Jacquou le Croquant*. Here is the novel which M. Rolland has tried to write. It is just the life, day by day, of a miller in Périgord —a man of strong political feeling, a democrat and a philosopher on his way, like Colas Breugnon. But the miller of the Frau, though rustic and plain-spoken, is not coarse, for his author lived all his life amid the peasants of Périgord and Quercy. The French peasant has his faults; he loves to excess his money and his land; but as a rule he is *not* coarse. I have known a great many, in the country, and, since the war, in hospital; but for coarseness commend me to the country folk of Zola, the man of letters; or those of the author of *Nono*, who is a schoolmaster; or these rowdy village folk of Romain Rolland's. They lay the rustic varnish on too thick. Beneath this vulgar varnish we discern an image sufficiently touching and quite in Romain Rolland's stoical vein : That of an obstinate, obdurate, wine-bibbing, and free-loving old cabinetmaker, besotted with his love of

xiv

art and liberty, who in the end, having lost his savings, his home, his wife, his sculptured treasures, finds himself happier than he ever was before (though bedridden, poor, and a pensioner in his children's bounty) because he has conquered the only liberty that really matters—the freedom of the soul.

It is impossible to suppose that *Colas Breugnon* will mark the close of M. Rolland's career. It is evidently a caprice, a *boutade*, an interlude. In what sense will his talent now develop? His years have just completed their half-century, but he still has some good autumns before him : Cervantes was turned fifty-seven when he published the First Part of *Don Quixote* !

To return to our Twentieth Century writers, Rostand stands the next upon our list. The war has neither augmented nor diminished Rostand. The few occasional poems that he published during its course are of slight importance; one imagines him following the tragic struggle with an attention so deeply engrossed that he half-forgot to breathe, and could not sing. When Victory promised us Peace, the strain relaxed. The fragile enthusiast could draw a deep breath. It was his last. He died, after a brief illness, a few weeks after the conclusion of the Armistice.

Let us turn the page again. Paul Claudel has written a few more dithyrambs in prose, but these five years have increased the volume without changing the character of his work. He is still predominantly the author of the *Cinq Grandes Odes*, of *L'Otage*, of *La Jeune Fille Violaine*, all published some years before the war. He serves his country as Consul in Brazil instead of at Hamburg; still in the full strength of his years, with doubtless other laurels to conquer, he stands out, among the ranks of our writers, a creature of passion and combat, active, emotional, mystic, and material at once—adequate to his age.

Francis Jammes, too, is unchanged, save by the natural process of the years. The Faun turned Friar is now more and more an author for the family circle. He is a candidate to the French Academy, which has just received his successor on our list, René Boylesve. This last writer, at least, has been deeply touched by the war. His fine novel, *Tu N'es Plus Rien*, will remain as evidence of that passionate patriotism—that detachment from all individual interests and, I might almost say, that cessation of all individual existence which made the France of the Great War as rapt, as ecstatic an example of the force of a collective sentiment as the France of the Great Revolution.

And now (after a passing glance at an unchanged, inconspicuous André Gide) we approach the name of Péguy. Péguy was killed in September, 1914, as he was leading his men into action at the Battle of the Marne. And as the flash of a fusee lights up the nocturnal battlefield, so that tragic illumination of his death reveals the true meaning of much that was obscure and easy to misunderstand in his gift. I own that I have almost entirely rewritten the chapter I had given to Péguy. I did not—do not—fully like or appreciate a genius now generally accepted as such in France, but I had composed my first sketch in a mood of freakish pleasantry, which might be permitted towards a man much younger than myself, with a great future before him, but which is not possible in speaking of a poet, dead, who died a martyr and a hero. It is perhaps the fault of a classical education which, if it was not very extensive at least sank deep, (inclining me especially to grace and measure, to something exquisitely right, exactly true)—it is perhaps the fault of a taste nourished on Sophocles and Plato that these ultra-lyrical modern geniuses, with their wild reiterations, their violence, their volume, their hoarse abundance, more often shock or dazzle me than please. . . . Péguy, Claudel, carry me off my feet, drown me, drench me in their billows full of sand and pebbles, and leave me gasping : 'Oh, for the well beneath the poplar in the field!' Yet Péguy and Claudel are the names which must be most profoundly considered in this little book, for they represent a generation. I have placed in Péguy's train, as witnesses and mourners, his friend Ernest Psichari, his fellow-officer, Émile Nolly, and the two really considerable writers who have risen into eminence during the war : Henri Barbusse and Georges Duhamel.

Three of our four ladies have passed through the

time of stress unscathed nor greatly left their impress on the angry world—not that they have not published in due course their poems or their novels. But these novels and poems are chiefly reflections from a mirror fully occupied by their own image. Madame Colette publishes to-day *Mitsou*; the tender irony and charming grace of her style are the same as of old—Mitsou is an enchanting little savage of the music-hall stage —Madame Tinayre has given us a novel which is an agreeable fresco of the day of mobilisation in Paris. Madame de Noailles has scattered a score of lyrics, like a handful of rose leaves and cypress-buds, over the pages of half a dozen reviews, but the terrible enigma—'Must I grow old like the others? And, if not, must I die?' is her most intimate preoccupation, and blurs in her eyes the great spectacle of the war.

Marie Lenéru nourished her soul in anguish on the tragic problem : How can it be that the most obvious social duty, the defence of hearth and home, should come to mean in practice, crime and cruelty let loose in the general reversal of all social law? The daughter of a line of sailors, with half a dozen *filleuls* in the Fusiliers-Marins, she was the most martial of pacifists, but also the most passionate. While embroidering a flag, or tying up a packet for the front, she was busy devising some League of Nations which might prevent the recurrence of the infernal storm. Early last spring she brought me to read a strange, violent, lyrical debate, rather than a play, which she had written. She called it *La Paix*, and hoped it might one day be performed before the Congress. She had wished, indeed, that the Théâtre Français should produce it instead of *La Triomphatrice*. But the House of Molière wisely stuck to its bargain : *La Paix* was not a piece for war-time.

La Triomphatrice appeared at the Théâtre Français in January, 1918. It did not take the town by storm. The play is too exclusively concerned with the manners and morals of a literary clique, and the question discussed is after all a very secondary question : Can a woman of genius be really happy and beloved as a woman—be as satisfactory as wife, mistress, or mother, as the more receptive non-creative sort? Marie Lenéru thought not. One feels inclined to answer that it does not really matter : there are so few women of genius. But Marie Lenéru debated her theme so passionately that it was impossible to turn an indifferent ear. If the general public remained aloof, the *salons* and the newspapers were full of *La Triomphatrice*, and recruited every week a wider audience. With Madame Bartet triumphant on the stage, with half the celebrities of Paris in the stalls, Marie Lenéru might feel her hour was come, or at least was at last tremblingly, exquisitely coming, in all its fullness. . . . She was ambitious. . . .

And then, on the 23rd of March, 'Grosse Bertha' began to thunder. The German shells fell in the

AFTERWORDS—AFTERWARDS

centre of Paris; on Good Friday a church was shattered, with all its faithful in it; one night, at the Français, actors and audience had to take refuge in the cellars, fortunately spacious. The theatre was closed. The play was stopped in mid-career. Mademoiselle Lenéru herself retired to Brittany. After a long summer's work and meditation, with more than one play filling her portfolio, she was full of plans for her winter in Paris, when she fell a victim to the epidemic of infectious influenza then devastating Lorient, and died there on the 23rd of September, 1918. Except Péguy, France has lost in the war no writer from whom we hoped a richer harvest. Some day we shall read *La Maison sur le Roc, Le Bonheur, La Paix*— those plays so full of thought and a sombre passion, which, to my thinking, are meant rather for the student's chair and the fireside lamp than for the glare of the footlights. A great, active, heroic soul still moves amply through all of them and swells their sails : may they carry down the stream of the century the echo of that voice, ardent and harsh, monotonous, and yet so strangely moving, which was silenced before it had time to deliver its full message.

No such rich promise was cut short by the death of André Lafon, who died of his wounds in hospital early in the war. A shepherd—that is how I see André Lafon—a charming young shepherd strolling down Mount Olympus, to whom the Muse gave, half-smiling, a dew-bespangled branch of laurel;

but, ere he could twist it into a crown, the wolf came ravening and made an end of him and it! It is not for his talent that I evoke the memory of André Lafon (though I have read and re-read *L'Elève Gilles* with singular sympathy, and love the too-slender, charming little book), but few things seem to me more romantic than the destiny of this young man. In the spring of 1912 a solitary, a sensitive, young usher in a school—before the year was out, his name on every lip, his purse swollen with those blessed ten thousand francs of the French Academy's new Great Prize (which he had wrested from Péguy), and his slim portfolio bursting with letters from publishers. He certainly was not a Byron (it generally is *not* the genius who 'wakes to find himself famous'); but that is always a romantic adventure, especially when, two years later, the young laureate fills a hero's grave. Had he a mother, still young, in some old house in the provinces, to glory in her son's miraculous achievement, and to mourn the withering of her hopes? I often sit and think of the fate of André Lafon—as delicate and sad as one of his own stories.

The name of Edmond Jaloux (nothing seems to have happened to the writers of Pastoral novels), reminds me that all our brilliant writers are not dead. He has certainly increased in value during the last five years. Two novels, published in 1918, but written on the eve of the war, *L'Incertaine* and *Fumées dans la Campagne*, prove him in full possession of his gift. His novels are exquisite impressions that somehow hauntingly convey the sense of something round the corner that might please us even more were it not just out of sight. *Fumées dans la Campagne*, especially, is a fine piece of work, subtle, tender, sad. Since *Le Reste est Silence*. M. Edmond Jaloux's art, while no less brilliant, has gained in depth and refinement. No writer on our list has in a higher degree the æsthetic sense. His landscapes breathe the very spirit of the South. The figures in them are gracious, cultivated beings, whose psychology is full of delicate sentimental complications. . . .

But his voice is the voice of yesterday—or at the latest of this morning : what will the morrow bring forth? The violent realism of Barbusse? the dithyrambs of Claudel? the infinitely delicate divagations of Marcel Proust? or something wholly different and unforeseen? With the signing of Peace we now enter a new era, and there will be new writers, doubtless, to greet the twentieth year of the Twentieth Century.

> Ultima Cumæi venit jam carminis ætas
> Magnus ab integro sæclorum nascitur ordo.

> Now dawns the last age of the Sybil's sooth,
> And lo ! the world, transformed, renews its
>   youth !

MARY DUCLAUX.

PARIS, *April*, 1919.

CONTENTS

MAURICE BARRÈS

I

MAURICE BARRÈS is the oldest of all the personages
of this little book, which deals emphatically with
the young—with the writers of the Twentieth
Century, and not with those already famous fifteen
years ago.   Still, every rule has its exceptions;
and it is impossible to imagine the young literature
of our days without this man of fifty.   Time flies,
and never did it seem to me to fly more swiftly
than in this moment, when I realise that Barrès
must be ranked among the middle-aged.   Only
the other day, he was that young Deputy, delight-
fully impertinent, impatient of the ways of his
elders, who rose from his bench in the Chamber
to propose 'that the ashes of Jules Simon be
transferred to the Panthéon'—Jules Simon being
at that moment comfortably seated in the Upper
House.   May it be long before the ashes of Maurice
Barrès are carried to the home of the immortals !

Yet Time has already begun his travesties :   the
Don Juan of letters, the *enfant terrible* of politics,
is already a sort of Conscript Father, almost· a
Father of the Church.   He, too, in the world of
letters, dignifies the Upper House, for he is an
Academician.   Maurice Barrès is the Chateaubriand

of our unfolding age, or, to translate my meaning into English, he is perhaps even more exactly its Disraeli—a Disraeli reversed : an incomparable artist, a brilliant politician, but, in this latter line, something of an amateur. Still we cannot imagine our Barrès stripped of his politics, nor even the literature of our time without the politics of Barrès. His Nationalism, his Regionalism fill and flood the literature of France as fully as Imperialism occupied the English horizons of yesterday. Doubtless we are moving out of the sphere of their influence. But they have nourished the imagination of our younger men.

The Barrès of the Nineteenth Century was less political. Like most of the masters of the present hour, he entered letters as a Symbolist, almost as a Decadent. Immersed in solitary introspection, he at first appeared as the Narcissus of the Inner Life, taking his stand somewhere between Bergson and Maeterlinck. In those days, he asked from politics merely an instigation, a fillip. That strange temperament of his, at once dreamy, lethargic, ironical and intensely passionate, sought in the tumult and the fatigues of Boulangism a spur and a sting, something which should urge and incite him to adventure. 'J'aime Boulanger,' he said, 'comme un stimulant.' Politics were for this young man an enchanting enterprise, an admirable expense of energy, an inward animation; and, even when he saw the General as he was, the experiment still seemed interesting and poignant.

Barrès was so weary of his own fastidious refinement that his devotion was perhaps enhanced by the discovery that his hero was just an average man. All that excitement and stir which his arid self-culture had not afforded him, he expected from the perpetual agitation of public life; he had exhausted (or thought he had exhausted, for he had not exterminated them from his brain) the philosophers and the mystics; he had done with Plotinus and Loyola and Hegel. Like the hero of *L'Ennemi des Lois*, he exclaimed :—

'Toujours les choses de l'intelligence ! Je les comprends; je n'en suis pas bouleversé. Ah ! des choses qui puissent changer les âmes !'

Barrès had delved down so deep into his conception of the Ego, that he had (so to speak) come out on the other side—at the Antipodes, and felt the need of merging himself in something larger and more durable than any individual existence. No longer the singular, the extraordinary, attracted him, but the normal type. And so, in General Boulanger, a certain pleasant vulgarity, a soldierly mediocrity of mind, seemed charming to this subtle neophyte : he recognised the quality—a cheap chromo-lithograph of Henri Quatre or Lafayette, and he liked his chief none the worse for it. He saved himself from smiling at his own enthusiasm by saying that Boulanger was just the captain to re-conquer Alsace-Lorraine for the French.

But, all the same, Boulanger was more to the

young member for Nancy than just a **glass of vermouth quaffed at the tavern door.** He soon saw that his adventurer was not adequate to the adventure; an absurd conspiracy ended in smoke. But when the last blue volutes had curled away, and left unchanged the face of the Republic, something important remained deposited in the mind of Maurice Barrès : the idea of a party which should embrace all opinions in its scheme for reform, a truly National party, bringing out of chaos a new organic order. Then he opened his Sophocles and pondered the magnificent line which no party leader has ever put in practice :—

οὔτοι συνέχθειν, ἀλλα συμφιλεῖν ἔφυν.

I live to share your loves and not your **hates.**

And through a maze of errors (for, in my opinion, the political adventures of Barrès were chiefly errors), this noble conception broadened and ripened, dignifying a patriotic traditionalism with such beauties as may spring from the hope of continuity and the sense of order.

A great gulf divides, as we shall see, the Barrès of the Nineteenth Century from the Barrès of the Twentieth. We will not consider in this place that earlier author, the gifted egoist of *Bérénice*, the anarchist of *L'Ennemi des Lois*, the lonely mystic of *L'Homme libre*, the dilettante, the self-worshipper. Let us merely say (in order to explain him) that our author was born in 1862 at Charmes in Lorraine, a man of a mingled race, with a strain of Teuton in him warring with the Celt, and a Rhenish sensibility hampered by a Latin love of rule and law. On his father's side, he traces his descent to Auvergne, and his relations still live in the little town of Mur-en-Barrez; but his mother's people all come from the neighbourhood of Nancy in Lorraine.

If we gave a free rein to our imagination, and let ourselves argue from type and talent to a strain of race, we might suppose that, like Montaigne, Barrès had in his stock some Jewish or Marrana grandmother, who gave him his taste for speculation, with something curious, double, and ironical in his outlook; but here, I believe, the genealogists protest.

His first impressions of conscious and public life were of a kind fit to aggravate the inherent melancholy of a sensitive and impassioned nature. He remembers a crowd, all surging towards one point under a hot summer sun, and that point the station; trains passing endlessly, filled with soldiers, thousands of soldiers, drunk, some with wine, some with sheer excitement, and all singing at the top of their voices. And the inhabitants of the little town of Charmes, men, women, and especially the little boys like himself, are striving towards, pressing against, hanging over the barriers and railings of the station, handing across bottles of wine, brandy, coffee, and crying: '*A Berlin!*' as loudly as the soldiers. And then a few weeks

later, the retreat : that day of stupefied astonishment in the soaking rain, while horsemen and
infantry in wild confusion troop by in a very rage
of shamed withdrawal; the soldiers insulting their
officers, a General in tears, the linen-clad Turcos
shivering in the dreary damp. And then five
Uhlans, their pistols in their hands, who ride
across the bridge and take possession.

The men of the Barrès family, notable citizens
of Charmes, were taken in hostage by the Prussians.
The trains that ran the Prussian troops towards
the front had a Barrès or so, as hostages, beside
the engine-driver. Their lives hung by a thread.
And so a proud, timid, melancholy little boy learned
early in life what it is to expect the worst, to go
in fear, and, out of pride, to dissimulate that fear.
The Nationalism of Barrès may be traced to these
first impressions. It is as invaders that he hates
the Germans : intellectually, he has no quarrel
with them.

In a discourse pronounced on the frontier during
the war-threatened summer of 1911, he asserted
anew all that he owes to the romantic fancy of
the Rhine, his real and fervent admiration for the
noble genius of Goethe, his tenderness for the
sentimental Schiller, his sense of a deep interior
affinity between his own mind and that of Nietzsche.
But those terrible memories of childhood have
graven in his spirit a certainty of the preciousness
(but also of the precariousness, the fragility) of
civilisation ; a hate and a contempt for the

'Barbarians' whose hordes are a perpetual menace; and a feeling that, though every nation has plenty of Barbarians at home, the worst of all Barbarians are the Prussian Uhlans and the Bavarian troopers of a German invasion.

Barrès was the most precocious, I think, of a generation that began to pierce the soil (so to speak) between 1886 and 1890, a generation idealist and sceptical at once, which counts among its glories Bergson, Maurras, Maeterlinck, and (their Benjamin) René Boylesve. At nineteen years of age, Barrès left Nancy and came up to Paris in order to study law : his deluded family hoped to make a magistrate of the 'Ennemi des Lois.'

But the dreamy youth, silent, timid, yet brilliant, had other aims in view. He had a volume of Schopenhauer in his pocket and a certain number of ideas in his head. He began to write in the young reviews and to show these first essays to his pastors and masters, the two rival librarians of the Senate, Leconte de Lisle and Anatole France. They were extraordinary essays which reflected in nothing the physiological naturalism of the hour—the hour of Zola! They were entirely, exaggeratedly spiritual and interior, and yet full of the dreariest nihilism. They were the essays of a man with a soul, who says in his heart : ' There is no God.'

Those early essays, those first novels, have nothing to do with the Barrès of the Twentieth Century, save inasmuch as the child is the father of the

man.   I have dealt with them elsewhere (in the
Quarterly Review), but some day it will be interesting
to take them up again and examine their development parallel to the philosophy of Bergson.   It
is often surprising, and makes one wonder if the
two writers have not, in their philosophy, some
common ancestor.   But who was he?   Was he
Burdeau?   Was he Ravaisson?   Was he Lachélier?
Was he Renouvier?

For my present purpose—which is to examine
the progress of Barrès, and especially his influence
on recent literature, it is enough to say that these
first volumes were the work of a man for whom
the inner world alone exists.   He, who was to
become the voice of his province and his race,
makes his first appearance as a being released from
all ties and all traditions.   The hero of *Sous l'oeil
des Barbares* has no country, no profession, no
family, no local habitation, and no name.   The
one existence and the one reality are, in his eyes,
the Ego,—in other words, his own mind.   His sole
adventure is the lonely courage of a descent into
that Inner Abyss.   He might have exclaimed with
Leopardi : ' E dolce, il naufragar in questo mare !'

In the depth of this depth is something deeper
still, continuous beneath the difference of individuals,
as the mass of the sea is one below the variety of
the waves.   'Penser solitairement, c'est s'acheminer
à penser solidairement,' Barrès exclaimed, half
ironically, in *Les Déracinés*.   If we sink deep
enough into our own souls, we fall into the general

soul of all : we find the deep subterranean flood that fills all the fountains of the city !

And so the Egoist discovers that he is not alone, that he is a living cell in a living organism. It is this sense of Life and solidarity which distinguishes Barrès, the man of action, Barrès, the political leader, Barrès, the inventor of Nationalism, the apostle of decentralisation, from the delightful nihilist, the exquisite anarchist, that he was at twenty—and even at thirty years of age. He has gone far since then ! Sure, now, of the existence of his race ; accompanied in all his thoughts by those mysterious cohorts of the dead and the unborn which prolong the importance of the humblest life; our philosopher bids us lay no stress upon our own experience, and sacrifice, if needs be, the details of our happiness to the welfare of the whole.

Slowly this second manner has developed since the closing years of the last century : between *L'Ennemi des Lois* (published in 1895) and *Les Déracinés* (1897) there is a chasm, an apparent disconnection. Something mysterious divides them —something akin to a religious conversion. What is the secret substratum which unites two phases evidently alike sincere? What makes their diversity none the less organic? It is, I think, *the sense of continuity*, the desire to persist and to preserve. The Barrès of *Les Déracinés* has reached the further edge of youth : he is five-and-thirty years of age.

Many men, on the threshold of forty, find themselves suddenly and terribly alone, in an hour of solemn solstice. So far, they have struggled up the hill gaily, with companions, and always have seen their goal ahead, like a cliff that shines in the sun and masks the horizon. Now on that topmost rock they stand, and now the road slopes downward—the road leading nowhere—which they must follow with diminished strength, in dwindling numbers, to find a tomb somewhere at the foot of the hill. Such an hour, such an experience marks for ever a sensitive nature. Some, then, like Tolstoi, have suddenly renewed the faith of their childhood and reconciled themselves with Christianity for the sake of a promised resurrection. Others build above the abyss a narrow bridge with the hope of the continuance of their race and their ideal. So Barrès will one day write :—

'J'ai confiance, pour atténuer certaines peines morales, dans un esprit fait de soumission à la terre natale, de fidélité aux morts, et de connaissance que tous nos actes entreront dans l'héritage social.' (*Amitiés Françaises*, p. 41.)

There is at Bar-le-Duc, in the church of Saint-Pierre, a mortuary statue of the Prince of Orange, by Ligier Richier, that tragic sculptor who left Lorraine to learn of Michael Angelo. The prince lies in the tomb, dead, in all the horror of corruption, his flesh dropping from his bones. But out of that appalling decomposition he lifts his heart intact—his living, his immortal heart—and he is reconciled to perish if that alone survive. So all of us, from the De Profundis of our accepted mortality, raise something we would fain bequeath as an heirloom to the future. Religion is based on such a sense of the persistence and the perpetuity of an ideal. Something, at least, survives; something is incorruptible; Sursum corda! and because of that persuasion of a continuity assured, the sadness of our own sure destruction is tempered with serenity and hope.

II

There exist two great families of literary works. One kind is complex, often diffuse, romantic, representing characters and sentiments too singular to be recognised save by the chosen few; of such are the works of Stendhal, and down to the close of the Nineteenth Century the novels of Barrès belong to this category. But in 1900, with *L'Appel au Soldat*, he will effect his transition to that other group, which instinctively we call classic, dealing with the simple sentiments of general humanity, seen from a great height, plumbed to a great depth. With *L'Appel au Soldat*, Barrès enters the sphere of Goethe.

If the book please me greatly, it is less for its animated picture of the Boulangist fever, for its

portrait of the General (so deeply pathetic in its
human weakness), less even for the death of Mme de
Bonnemains (though few things are more heartrending) than for an interlude of some seven score
pages, *La Vallée de la Moselle,* the simple account
of a bicycle tour taken by two young men, natives
of Lorraine, from Bar-le-Duc in France to Coblenz,
which once was France.   But these chapters are
written with a freshness and a feeling, a flexibility,
an evident sincerity which make them infinitely
touching.   That Spanish crudity, bizarre, elliptic,
which Barrès used to affect, has vanished here.   A
romantic sentiment is expressed with the ripe calm
and in the pure language of a classic.   Our Barrès
sails his black Venetian gondola along the most
harmonious, amplest stream.   He has forgotten
his impertinence and his perversity, but he has
lost nothing of his grace.

Marriage and the birth of a son had, no doubt,
much to do with this happy evolution. To a man
haunted by the dread of annihilation, a child is
an assurance against complete extinction.   He is
(as the Parsees say in their touching phrase) 'a
bridge' : a bridge across the abyss. A child pro-
longs our Ego and assures the continuity of all that
we inherit from our ancestors.   A child, we may say,
is the printed proof of our manuscript, safe henceforth, and no longer so unique or so important !

The volume which Barrès wrote for his little
son of six years old is a sunlit exception in his
writings, as a rule so profoundly melancholy. *Les*

Amitiés Françaises is a First Reader in patriotism, an alphabet of honour. It is an exquisite book and might take for an epigraph the motto of the town of Toul : *Pia, pura, fidelis.* It is the notebook of an observer who is a poet, of a poet who is a philosopher, of a philosopher who is a father; yet even here I distinguish that subtle, poignant note of suffering egotism, as inseparable from Barrès' work as from that of Chateaubriand. There are moments (as in the anecdote called *Le Trou*) when this mournful undertone rises almost to the pitch of rancour—a rancour almost immediately caught up, it is true, in a passion of tenderness and gratitude. The child, Philippe, shall see the light of the sun so many years after the abyss shall have swallowed up the father !

'Non, Philippe, tu ne glisseras dans le trou que trente années après que j'y serai—vingt années après que ta petite maman y sera. Tant je que demeurerai, jamais Philippe n'ira dans le trou !'

And the same passionate prolongation shows itself at another moment in a tender encroachment, a yearning monopoly, as though the father would engross and captivate the child and make him his, nay, make him *he !*—pour into this new vial the old wine of his own heart, fill the transparent and unsullied vase with the precious vintage which it shall carry safely for one more season, decanted, as it were, from one vessel into another. The child

is a new lease of life; the child is a bath of renewal;
new eyes wherewith to see things in the old forgotten glamour; new ears with which to hear
delicate sounds that this long while have escaped
the father's thickening tissues; above all the child
is an innocence, a freshness unspeakable :—

'Tu vis chacune de mes heures. Avec toi je
repasserai par mon humble sentier. Ô ma jeunesse,
ma plus bête et jeune jeunesse, qui refleurit !
Quand j'étais rassasié, voilà que, par cet enfant,
je me retrouve à jeûne devant le vaste univers.'

This paterfamilias had been the most passionate
of pilgrims. Under the correctness and irony of
his style there had trembled an exasperated sensibility. Impassioned and methodical, enthusiastic
and circumspect, chimerical and positive, two
natures had warred in Barrès; their conflict had
been at once his torment and his delight; and the
most romantic of European landscapes had long
been the battlefield of their interior quarrel. On
the red and sunburned hills of Toledo, Barrès
had mused on the cruelty of sensual passion and
on the imminence of death; he had meditated in
the cathedral and had read the inscription on a
pavement at his feet : 'Hic jacet pulvis, cinis, et
nihil.' And Venice had dissolved in his veins her
enervating beauty. But now it was towards
Sparta that he took the road. The very title is
a programme—*Le Voyage de Sparte !* (1906).

Of all the glorious memories of Greece there is
nothing that so much attracts our traveller as the
memory of two foreign visitors—Chateaubriand
and Lord Byron; the pathetic rather than the
heroic remains his ideal still. Yet little by little
Athena draws his soul towards her; first by
Antigone, a figure at once pathetic and heroic,
faithful to her dead, a holocaust to her race; and
next by the tombs of Greece, sepulchres carved
over with images of beauty and regret, yet without
despair or anguish. They teach that calm acceptance of the inevitable which is more than resigna-
tion, which is serenity.

And one day, on the banks of the Eurotas, Barrès
discovers a form of beauty novel to his soul, made
of measure and ease and grace, without excess
or rapture. 'On y trouve des beautés que l'on
peut aimer sans souffrir!' The sense of the whole,
the acceptance of the inevitable, the tranquilness
of Art, 'épuré de tous éléments de désespoir,'
these are conceptions which, if properly assimilated,
are a liberal education for a Romantic. Barrès
could not say, like Gautier, 'La vue du Parthénon
m'a guéri de la maladie gothique;' the process
was slow and painful, and the inoculation of the
antique was followed by a violent and feverish
reaction. Between him and that unequalled past
there is a solution of continuity; it is a perfection
into which he cannot enter, for lack of a few
drops of Greek blood in his veins; yet he has
had his lesson, which he will not forget, and

bears away with him a counsel to ponder in his heart.

'La déesse m'a donné, comme à tous ses pèlerins, le dégoût de l'enflure dans l'art. Il y avait une erreur dans ma manière d'interpréter ce que j'admirais; je cherchais un effet, je tournais autour des choses jusqu'à ce qu'elles parussent le fournir. Aujourd'hui j'aborde la vie avec plus de familiarité, et je désire la voir avec des yeux aussi peu faiseurs de complexités théâtrales que l'étaient des yeux grecs.'

In this new mood of simplicity and responsibility, Barrès conceived two short novels, companion pictures, lessons in civic virtue; one for a man, the other for a girl: *Au Service de L'Allemagne* (1905), and *Colette Baudoche* (1909). The theme of the first occurs already in *L'Appel au Soldat*, where the two heroes examine the situation of a young French Lorrainer under a German government. When the hour comes for his military service, shall the young man desert across the frontier to a land where he is scarce accounted French, or drafted off into the Légion Étrangère? Or shall he bow the neck to the usurper? And to whom shall he owe allegiance in case of war: France or Germany?

The hero of *Au Service de L'Allemagne* is a young Alsatian, whose very name is a symbol: Ehrmann, the man of honour. He is the son of one of those old autochthonous families who, under German rule, remain at heart profoundly French; whose ancestors have fought the battles of Louis Quatorze and Napoleon; who continue to talk French by their own fireside. In Alsace-Lorraine they are at home; in France, almost as much as in Germany, they are across the border. The French novelist has hitherto taken for granted that his hero should *opter pour la France*; yet in this fashion, without great profit to the mother country, Alsace-Lorraine is being emptied of her French blood.

Let the Alsatian serve his time in a German regiment, says Maurice Barrès; and, afterwards, let him live his life as an Alsatian doctor among Alsatian patients; as an Alsatian manufacturer among Alsatian workmen; let him remain true to 'La Terre et les Morts!' Let him march in the ranks with comrades who may be the foes of to-morrow, for his first duty is neither to Germany, which has annexed him against his will, nor to France, which stirs not a finger to let him out of prison, but to Alsace-Lorraine, the home of his race. So Ehrmann invents a new casuistry which, in an impossible situation, satisfies his conscience : he will serve his time in a German corps, reserving the right to desert in case of a war with France. But, even in that extremity, he will be no spy; he will reveal no secret learned during the time of compulsory service; he will observe towards his old colours a loyalty absolute while it lasts, which shall be succeeded by a faithful silence.

The sacrifice of Colette Baudoche, if not more difficult or more meritorious, is simpler and easier to admire. There lives in an old house at Metz an old *bourgeoise*, Madame Baudoche, the widow of a land agent, and her young orphaned granddaughter, Colette. To eke out their narrow means, the two women do a little dressmaking among the neighbours who have known them in happier days, and let their two front rooms. Enters to them a young Prussian schoolmaster at the Lycée (the 'gymnasium'), and he becomes their lodger. Asmus is a good young bear, a friendly and cordial young bore. It is his first contact with the Spirit of France—with ease, measure, liberty, and grace —qualities which the young German begins by admiring as French, but soon ends by loving as peculiar to Colette Baudoche.

Asmus is the most generous of conquerors, for his heart is filled by a tender admiration for the vanquished. He listens to, looks at, admires all that springs from the trampled soil. His love of Nature—which at first is vague and pantheistic —takes on the tone of France and becomes human, historical, and scientific. His rich but rough nature acquires finer shades and subtler blendings; in fact, little by little, Lorraine recreates the German tyrant in her own image :—

'Il y a des petits villages, isolés au milieu des espaces ruraux, qui, le soir, à l'heure où l'on voit rentrer les bêtes et les gens, m'apparaissent comme

des gaufriers; et je crois que tout être, fût il
barbare prussien, soumis à leur action patiente
et persistante, y deviendrait lentement Lorrain.
Bien des générations reposent là, au cimetière,
mais leur activité persiste; elle est devenue ce
groupe de maisons, ce clocher, cet abreuvoir, cette
école qu'entourent les champs bigarrés de couleurs
et de formes; et si l'on entre dans cette communauté,
on y vient nécessairement à se conduire et penser
comme ont fait les prédécesseurs.'

On Herr Doktor Friedrich Asmus the land of
Lorraine exercises this sort of transformation the
more readily that he adores Colette; and she is
touched by his loyalty and strength. Nature
pushes her into his arms; and old Madame Baudoche
can only sigh and say, 'C'est bien dommage qu'il soit
Allemand !' The excellent young man sets out on
his summer holidays almost sure of Colette's accord.
But she is a young maid of the lineage of Corneille,
accustomed to poise her feelings, and to decide
less by a passion of the heart than by a free consent
of the mind. For the whole world, she would not
forfeit her sense of honour ! And Asmus returns
on Commemoration Day, when all that is French
in Metz is met together to attend a service in
memory of the soldiers of France fallen during
the siege. During that service something larger
than herself takes possession of the heart and soul
of the little dressmaker. 'Elle se sent chargée
d'une grande dignité, soulevée vers quelque chose

de plus vaste, de plus haut et de plus constant que sa modeste personne.' Coming out of church she turns to the kind and fervent young Prussian who accompanies her : 'Monsieur le docteur, dit la jeune fille, je ne peux vous épouser.'

Maurice Barrès also is like his heroic Colette. 'Il se sent chargé d'une grande dignité, soulevé vers quelque chose de plus vaste, de plus haut, et de plus constant que sa personne.' He has gone far since first we met him, half-mystical, half-quizzical, rapt in the cult of the Ego. Now, as we have said, freed from the service of Self, 'La Terre et les Morts' is his watchword.

III

Or rather 'La Terre et les Morts' *was* his watch-word, for of late years the Dead have revealed to him something wider and deeper than the Land. Let us compare with the perverse charm and insidious nihilism of his earlier book on Toledo, *Du Sang, de la Volupté et de la Mort* (1895), his treatment of the same theme in his recent essay on Il Greco, and we shall catch the difference. In either volume the landscape is the same. The scene is arid; the red, steep banks of the ravine through which the Tagus rolls its tawny floods lead to a city set in ruin upon its lofty rocks; no site suggests a more ardent melancholy.

In his young days, Maurice Barrès declared that

the traveller entering Toledo tasted the same harsh
and acrid pleasure that he derived from reading
Pascal's *Pensées* or from contemplating Michael-
Angelo's *Penseroso* : in three gulps, it is the same
rough and heroic draught. The melancholy splendour of the scene exaggerates the stranger's sense
of loneliness. There is an implacable indifference
to his needs in these magnificent ruins, and the
yellow rocks repeat the strange device inscribed
upon a brass let into the floor of the Cathedral.
Twenty years ago, this device appeared, in the
eyes of Barrès, to declare the secret of the city.
They are singular words to adorn a Christian
tomb : *His jacet pulvis, cinis, et nihil.*

But see how differently in 1910 our traveller
will read the secret of Toledo ! Now, as of old,
the city on its sun-baked height, with the tawny
semicircle of the Tagus at its feet, seems less a
dwelling for men than a dreary highplace of the
soul, a sanctuary set apart for spiritual exaltation.
The dry orange tone of the soil and buildings; the
town compact of convents, fortresses, and prisons;
the barren sublimity of the prospect; the violent
African heat of the sky; the vast scent of sun-dried
lavender and sage and benjoin, seem proper to
some Holy City of the desert rather than to a
European town. And yet in all this sadness there
is a secret pleasure.

'J'y respire une volupté dont j'ignore le nom,
et quelque chose comme un péché se mêle à tout

un passé d'amour, d'honneur et de religion. C'est
le mystère de Tolède, et nous voudrions le
saisir. Mais que donc pourrait nous guider?
Toute société a fui de cette ruine impériale.'

A painter, long dead, a foreigner—Il Greco—is
the traveller's guide. It sometimes happens that
a foreigner surprises the fine evasive spirit of a
place which escapes the native, staled by custom,
until he catch it again through the fresh acuity of
a stranger's glance. It was the Fleming, Philippe
de Champagne, newly disembarked from Brussels,
who discerned the austere heroism of Port-Royal;
and a Greek from Candy came from Venice to
Toledo in his twentieth year to surprise the secret
of Spain. He painted the souls of the men and
women who breathed the same air as Saint Teresa
and Cervantes.

Through him we learn the secret of Toledo,
and Barrès will no longer tell us that it is the
dreary motto: *Pulvis, cinis, et Nihil;* nay, he
assures us now that it is the mystical world beyond
reality—the spiritual life. The Cretan painted the
serious, narrow faces, the bizarre, aristocratic,
and elongated persons of his sitters, but also the
constant object of their secret thought: that
wonderful, mysterious, illimitable Other-World,
urging and surging just on the further side of
appearances; a world to which they aspire, and
ascend, which seems to suck them up into the
eddying whirlpool of the glorious Unseen.

He loves to paint a double vision : on the lower half of his canvas Il Greco sets the world he knows : the men of sad and sober visage, of neat features and pointed beards and ruffs, elegant, honourable gentlemen; scarcely, perhaps, men of a great capacity; and then above them, only just barely overhead, a mad world (if you choose to call it mad) a mystical world at any rate, of rushing spirits, of flooding light, of joy and fire (*Joie! Joie! Joie! Pleurs de joie!*), a world of adoration, bliss, eternal peace.

'Et l'on a dit qu'il était fou ! . . . Attention ! Tout simplement, c'est un catholique espagnol. . . . Ses toiles complètent les traités de Sainte Thérèse et les poèmes de Saint Jean de la Croix. Elles initient à la vie intérieure des dignes Castillans. Aucun livre n'en donne une idée aussi compléte, aussi neuve.'

The faults of Il Greco, his voluntary distortion of the figures that he represents, their flame-like fragility and aspiration, the lividness of the painter's palette are not repugnant to our critic, who is always willing to permit a sacrifice of exterior truth in order to obtain a greater intensity of expression. The admirer of Ligier Richier may well be tender to the errors of Il Greco; fortunate errors, since they are perhaps a condition of the utterance of a certain spiritual state :—

'De tels états ne semblent pas compatibles avec
la grande civilisation et par exemple avec l'emploi
de chef de gare. Mais ils laissent dans Tolède une
atmosphere où plus d'un, qui ne s'en doute pas,
gagnerait à fréquenter.'

More and more the consideration of these spiritual
conditions will henceforth absorb the attention of
Maurice Barrès. The indulgent historian of Bérénice,
the heir of Montaigne, has gradually become the
attentive devotee of Pascal, the commentator of
L'Angoisse de Pascal; for Pascal, all sincerity and
force and fire, attracts the myriad-minded, the
dilettante Barrès. As he has surprised the secret
of Toledo, so would he master the mystery of this
great savant who made so light of science.

There are points of resemblance between Barrès
and Pascal : both are sons of Auvergne, with something positive and exact in their imagination, a
keen grasp of facts, a hatred of conventions. In
Pascal also, though so fiery on occasion, there is
something cold and harsh. And he, too, knew that
amor dominandi which so often inspired the political
combats of Barrès; Pascal, too, in his youth, was
imperious, vivacious, full of bizarre melancholy;
he, likewise, had been a dreamer and a dilettante.
And though the ultimate character of Pascal was
a tragic spiritual grandeur, yet almost to the end
there was a freakishness mixed up with it, a love
of paradox, a delight in subterfuges and disguises.
Saint as he was, Pascal was prompt to disdain,

Maurice Barrès

To face p. 24

proud, full of self-confidence, ardent; he had his
vanities and curiosities. His passionate and avid
soul was often unsatisfied, 'parce que ce gouffre
infini ne peut-être rempli que par un objet infini
et immuable, c'est à dire, par Dieu même.' (*Pensées*,
p. 425.)

Was it the memory of Pascal that inclined Barrès
to collect the fragmentary legends and souvenirs,
even the documents, of a humbler mystic, half
saint and half schismatic, once famous in the region
round Charmes, the little town where Barrès was
born and where he still spends his summers?

Perhaps; but Barrès (whose singular temperament appears to combine the sense of order with
a contempt for law) has always sought an axiom, a
religion, a discipline, which would satisfy an ardent
sensibility, and unite the individual with the
brothers of his race and faith, while yet leaving
free that inner Ego which, after all, has nothing
to do with our organisations and arrangements,
which transcends reason and order, being (if indeed
anything is) in direct communication with the
Infinite. From the time he wrote *Un Homme
Libre*, from the time he organised Nationalism,
Barrès has always sought a rule and a regulation;
but he has never bowed his head to a yoke. Self-
discipline, not obedience, is what he sought—and
at one season he sought it in the ascetic life. But
we must not forget that ἀσκητής means an athlete,
one who has exercised himself and grown strong;
and that which Barrès has always desired, in

religion as in politics, is a perfecting and augmenting of his own personality.

That way lies heresy ! And a heretic is the hero of Barrès' last novel, *La Colline Inspirée.*

It is a narration of religious experience (or rather of religious aberration), and at the same time it is an idyll of a strange Druid-like poetry, all the native sap and strength of Celtic forests and high places. Chateaubriand, with his Velléda, Renan, these alone in France have touched that deepest fibre of the Celtic heart, that dread, sacred, and yet sweet, that sense of communion with the Invisible, of which the mystery is deeper than the baptismal font and larger than the consecrated altar stone. Rome will never entirely wean Barrès from his devotion to the Celtic divinities of wood and weald. In *La Colline Inspirée* he opposes Poetry and Dogma. On the one hand, the Church, with its venerated hierarchy, its discipline, its universality and order; on the other, the mystic, the prophet —impatient of all mediation between the instinct of his soul and the eternal life—the seer of visions, too often sensual or insane.

Léopold Baillard is a real personage—almost contemporary, since he died in 1883. He and his two brothers, born of pious peasants in the dawn of the Nineteenth Century were three priests who dreamed of restoring, not only in their invisible supremacy but also in their positive and material prosperity, the prestige and the power of the native shrines of Lorraine. They were, in fact, as we should say (only a hundred years too soon), Celtic revivalists. Restorers of altars fallen into decay, founders of religious congregations, they were, during the first years of their ministry, th pride and the miracle of Alsace as of Lorraine. The acropolis of Sainte Odile in the Vosges and the sanctuary of Sion-Vaudémont in Lorraine became the property of Léopold Baillard and his brothers, where they founded convents and hostelries, and instituted an Order of Begging Sisters, who travelled all over Europe collecting alms. (A happy touch is that which shows Léopold Baillard in the Imperial Palace at Vienna, asking a contribution from the Emperor of Austria as Count de Vaudémont in Lorraine.)

Their enterprise, their intrepid imagination, their financial audacities awakened the mistrust of a prudent bishop, who refused to confirm the miraculous cure of one of the Sisters, and subsequently withdrew his sanction from their quest of alms. It was the axe-stroke at the root of the Baillards' prosperity; it was the deliberate quashing of a new (but a less spiritual) Port Royal. The Baillards were obliged to sell all their possessions, and, bankrupt in purse and credit, they were sent into retreat in a Cistercian monastery. In that place of peace a Cistercian father inconsiderately bade Léopold Baillard visit in Normandy a wonder-working visionary, Vintras, a prophet in his degree.

Baillard was a sort of romantic genius—the

genius of revolt and sentiment—a man for whom
the invisible world exists so naturally that nothing
in him protested when Vintras, on the occasion
of their meeting, declared himself in constant and
direct communication with a spiritual sphere.
Baillard returned from Normandy to Sion-Vaudémont a fervent disciple of the New Elias (as Vintras
styled himself), and, on the scene of his old labours,
began to edify—with how much less success !—
a schismatic Church.   But he is no longer the
prosperous, the genial, Abbé Léopold Baillard.
His cure is taken from him, his doctrines are condemned, his person excommunicated.   He is the
fallen Angel, he whom pride misled.

There is tenderness as well as irony, poetry as
well as tragedy, deep compassion mixed with a
half-reluctant disapproval in the eloquence of M.
Barrès, as he relates the downfall of the schismatic
—his follies, his errors, his sufferings, his long
martyrdom, his final reconciliation with the Church.
Melius est ut pereat unus quam unitas.   Yet if
that one be Pascal, or Fénelon, or Father Tyrrell,
or even an Abbé Léopold Baillard (so mere a
peasant in his harsh materialism, so nearly a saint
in his inspired spirituality), how shall one not
admire the ardour, the grandeur, the genius, the
generosity of a soul superior to the docile flock?
The lost sheep (depend upon it) was the fairest of
the fold—and was, as we know, the dearest to the
immortal Shepherd.   The sympathies, if not the
convictions, of the author are evidently with the

vanquished prophet. For a religion, says our author, is made of two elements, with difficulty conciliable, yet equally vital: on the one hand, enthusiasm, inspiration; on the other, discipline, authority.

'Eternel dialogue de ces deux puissances! A laquelle obéir? Et faut-il donc choisir entre elles? Ah! plutôt qu'elles puissent, ces deux forces antagonistes, s'éprouver éternellement, ne jamais se vaincre et s'amplifier par leur lutte même. Elles ne sauraient se passer l'une de l'autre. Qu'est-ce qu'un enthousiasme qui demeure une fantaisie individuelle? Qu'est-ce qu'un ordre qu'aucun enthousiasme ne vient plus animer?'

Est aliquid hominis quod nec ipse scit spiritus hominis qui in ipso est: there is more in man than the soul of man conceives. This line of Saint Augustine (which serves as an epigraph to *La Colline Inspirée*) might be inscribed above all Maurice Barrès' later writings: they are all laid on the altar of an Unknown God. Nothing in the eyes of this barely orthodox critic is more sacred, more moving than a village church, whose narrow chancel has echoed the prayers, the praise, of countless spirits straining to approach the secret Reality which sustains the world of Appearances. The stones have witnessed the tears of generations many times renewed as they consigned their dead to the keeping of God; before the same altar

fathers and children have plighted their troth;
and the font served to christen the grandsires of
to-day. A village church is, to an imaginative
mind, a thing which revives the sacred memory
of our country and our dead. And so—not in a
spirit of narrow orthodoxy—but in the largest and
most human movement of generosity—Barrès takes
up his pen to plead for the churches of France,
falling into ruin since the separation of Church
and State.

It must be remembered that, when these parted
company, there was a question of constituting
certain parish councils, or *associations cultuelles*,
specially charged with the maintenance of the
churches of France; but the Vatican, ever sus-
picious of all that tends towards a decentralisation
of authority, would not allow of their existence.
In consequence, no responsibility towards the
Government obliges the communes to restore their
parish church; if it fall into disrepair, they may
abandon it or amend it at their own sweet will,
should it threaten to tumble about their shoulders,
they may disaffect it, or even at a last extremity,
pull it down altogether.

Now, such is the antagonism of free-thinker and
Catholic in France, especially in the less cultivated
part of the community, that in certain villages,
where the Church-people would be willing to
restore their parish church at their own expense,
a sectarian town council has forbidden them to
do so, and, by an abuse of authority, has declared

the church disaffected. In other hamlets, too poor for so great an outlay, the church is in ruins for lack of means and initiative. In others, their treasure, however slight, of old glass, enamel, tapestry, or gold and silver embroideries, old lace, or mediæval carving, has awakened the cupidity of those who know too well how to dispose of such relics of the past.

It is true that certain churches and certain treasures are considered worthy of the rank of historical monuments, and, as such, are entrusted to the protection of the State. But the thesis of M. Barrès is that *all* churches, built before 1800 (I don't know why he insists upon the date), should be included in this immunity; that any vote of a sum to be expended in repairs, decreed by a commune or department, should be immediately doubled by the Government; and that any ratepayer should have the right to restore his parish church at his own expense. It is not as a Catholic that he pleads the cause of the altar, but in the name of civilisation; and he requires the nation to repair its village churches just as he would demand the preservation of the National Library or the College of France.

'C'est à la civilisation qu'il faut s'intéresser, si l'on n'a pas le sens de Dieu et si l'on est rassasié du moi. Eh bien! la civilisation, où est-elle défendue aujourd'hui?'

'Dans les conseils d'administration? Je ne suis

pas de ceux qui le croient. Elle est défendue dans les laboratoires et dans les églises.'

It is perhaps a little difficult to formulate the intellectual position of Barrès. What he craves, appears to be, not an orthodoxy, but a preserve of Mystery; a sort of private hunting ground for the imagination; the right to lean out of the visible world and draw a deep breath, *hors de la prison des choses claires.* Or, shall we say? in the blank wall of our science and our ignorance, he wants to be free to throw open a window looking on the Infinite? He defends, perhaps, less a faith than a conception of life which is bound up with all our ideas of honour, our notions of sacrifice. I think he is inspired by a sense of ancestral piety rather than by what we usually term religion. Indeed, I imagine that no reader would have more intimately vibrated to *La Grande Pitié des Èglises de France*, than a certain old friend of mine, whom Barrès did not always understand, by name Ernest Renan—Renan who wrote (already in 1849) :—

'N'y aurait il quelque moyen d'être catholique sans croire au catholicisme?'

And who are the followers whom Barrès calls to the rescue against an excess of sectarian zeal —against the village science of the Radical druggist, of Monsieur Homais? Nothing is more interesting, more symptomatic, to those who remember the France of yesterday, when, as a rule, the Intellectuals and the artists were on one side of the hedge, and the priests and the pious on the other. Persecution has certainly done wonders for the Church in France! Those whom Maurice Barrès convokes to defend the belfry and the altar are the younger generation in letters!

'Je ne doute pas de leurs réponses. . . . Ces mêmes jeunes troupes désintéressées qui auraient à d'autres moments, combattu, rejeté un catholicisme oppressif . . . se rassemblent d'instinct pour faire face à la Barbarie. Je voudrais tracer içi le tableau de la littérature nouvelle que je salue et d'où s'élève, plus ou moins haut, la grande flamme spirituelle que le Café du Commerce ne voit pas. . . .'

ROMAIN ROLLAND

AMONG the still young masters of the young in France, the men rising fifty—Rostand, Claudel, Boylesve, Gide, Suarès, Francis Jammes, Romain Rolland—only the first and the last are really well known beyond our frontiers. Claudel is appreciated in Germany as an interesting exotic; but there, as well as in England and Italy, Romain Rolland has an audience of his own. In some ways he is the most approachable of French writers to an English, or, indeed, to an Italian mind. His intense moral earnestness, his love of nature, his lack of irony, and his sense of sarcasm, no less than an idealism devoid of all religiosity, distinguish him among the men of his generation. And he is an Individualist. When Claudel gibes at the idols which Freethinkers raise on their altars—the geniuses and the heroes, all the great men—be sure he is thinking of Romain Rolland, and perhaps of Suarès. Hero-worship, love of the poor and humble, faith in the human mind and its divine destinies, are indeed, to Romain Rolland, as much a religion as the doctrines of the Catholic Church to Claudel, or to his convert, Francis Jammes.

Romain Rolland owes his fame to *Jean-Christophe*, his great novel in ten volumes, the *Clarissa* of our

age. But he has written many other books. Romain
Rolland's unknown works are voluminous and
abundant. Some twenty years ago I used to take
them to the *Revue de Paris* and expend all my
small store of diplomacy in persuading the editor
to print those immense and formless dramas,
Saint Louis, Aert, Danton, in which rare streaks of
real genius illumined desolate wastes of verbiage.
I cannot say that any of them attained success.

Having striven to express his mind in these
inchoate symphonies, Romain Rolland tried a
new form of art, in which from the first
stroke he was singularly successful : his *Lives of
Great Men* (*Vies des Hommes Illustres*), have the
terseness, the morality, the grandeur, and the
natural piety of Plutarch's *Lives*. He has written
nothing better than his *Beethoven* or his *Michael
Angelo*, and he has given us a *Mazzini*, a *Tolstoi*
only less excellent. These are quite little books,
so far as size is concerned. And the mind of Romain
Rolland continued to teem with images and ideas,
with a sense of the tragedy of human destiny, and
yet with an invincible hope in human reason. He
had a thousand things to say to the men of his
generation; his heart burned within him. So he
invented a great man of his own making, Jean-
Christophe.

Here he has written the tragedy of a free soul,
the tragedy rather, let us say, of a whole generation
perpetually in quest of Truth and Liberty. There
are many stars in the sky; there are many virtues

in the soul of man; perhaps no two succeeding
generations make their idols of the same. Truth,
Justice, Freedom, inflamed our youth with a noble
passion. The young men of to-day adore Courage,
Activity, Self-control, and Faith. They are optim-
ists. We were pessimists. And Romain Rolland
writes, as a foreword to the tenth volume of his
novel :—

'I have written the tragedy of a generation which
soon must disappear. I have sought to dissimulate
nothing of its vices or its virtues—neither its
heavy sadness, its chaotic pride, its heroic efforts,
nor its spent weariness under the crushing burden
of a superhuman task : for we had to renew our
whole epitome of life, our conception of the world,
our æsthetics and our ethics, our religion, our
humanity.'

A Hamlet-like generation, intensely intellectual,
sensitive, and chivalrous, issuing painfully from the
shed sheath of a worn-out creed and struggling
painfully towards a loftier faith and a fuller life
—such is the subject of *Jean-Christophe*. And the
author, merely middle-aged, has lived to see a new
race inherit the earth : a race ingenuous, ingenious,
active, alert, little given to self-questioning, or
to any form of subtlety, and as a rule content with
the religion of its forefathers, just because it was
the religion of one's forefather's, and is probably
as good as any other. Already *Jean-Christophe* is

a portrait of the past, and certain volumes—as a
rule those we admired the most on their appearance : for instance *La Foire sur la Place*—present
the half-pathetic interest of a photograph album
ten years old.

What is still fresh, what is still moving and
touching and delightful is the story of a heart,
the painting of passion and especially the drawing
of the feminine figures—the very numerous feminine
figures—who diversify the existence of Jean-
Christophe.

The novel has been translated into English.
My readers know (or at least can easily learn)
that the story is that of a great German musician.
It follows him from his childhood in a little Rhenish
town, to Paris, whither Jean-Christophe resorts,
when, after a skirmish with a Prussian officer,
he has to flee for his life across the frontier. There
is no plot. The story is as ill-defined, as vague,
as fluctuating, as constantly developing, as life
itself ; and these ten volumes are a sequence of
episodes rather than a tale. Above all, they are a
criticism of contemporary Europe, or rather of the
Europe of yesterday, a Europe less infected with
Nationalism, Imperialism, Panslavism, than the
instable and agitated compound that we know.

The hero is born in Germany. No German book,
I think, not even *Werther*, gives with a sweeter
serenity, the peculiar charm of Rhenish 'Gemüth-
lichkeit' than these early volumes of *Jean-Christophe*.
But, as the hero grows older, he finds himself

constantly hostile to the dreamy optimism of his environment. He hates the humbler forms of German idealism—that public and private Pharisee-ism which will not admit the world to be that which it is; the majestic sentimentality which invades all German art; that general artifice of emotion, moral nobleness, sensibility, and poetry which exasperates when it does not endear.

Even the 'cher vieux Schultz,' 'le bon Alle-mand,' Christophe's one admirer; even Modesta, the blind girl who will not allow that she has any cause to be unhappy, irritate the choleric young man, despite their candid goodness and their tranquil courage, because of a certain unconscious hypocrisy in their attitude, a habit of ignoring the truth when it happens to be disagreeable. Christophe cannot as yet admit that human nature is incapable of assimilating unadulterated reality : he has still to learn that every nation mixes with the truth some special spice of lies; and that there are more dangerous condiments than a romantic optimism. He himself, in his cult of force, is no less local, no less German : he is merely a German of a later generation.

When Christophe flies to France, he finds to his discomfiture that sincerity is not a common attribute, even across the frontier; but French insincerity is of a different sort, cynical, excitable. France has ever been a *fanfaron de vices*, and loves to brag of her depravity rather than to practise it. The angry, heady, passionate, fuming youth spares no class or type in his first revolt against his new environment : the squalor of the poor, the struggling ambition and snobbish meannesses of the world of art, the hollow ceremony of fashionable circles combine to make him hate Paris. Little by little he penetrates below the surface : his friend Olivier Jalin interprets to him the real France. The intellectuals and the æsthetes of twenty years ago, who so irritate Christophe on his first arrival, were but the foam on the face of a deep reality. 'C'est curieux que vous soyez Française !' says the musician to his friend's sister, with her honest, girlish face, her round, full forehead, her little straight nose, her neat small chin, and the brown locks that frame so demurely her thin cheeks.

This quiet little girl, at once artless and disenchanted, pious and disillusioned, does not answer in the least to the conception that a young German artist forms of France. But we know better ! The little governess personifies that France, known to few outside her boundaries, which is compact of sacrifice, of duty, of delicate conscientiousness, of rigid economy for self and generous outlay for some treasured ideal, child, or cause :—the France of Port-Royal, the France of '48. Indeed, if we mistake not, Mademoiselle Antoinette Jeannin has misspelt her name; and we envy the novelist who (annihilating time and space) can link the mind of Beethoven to the soul of Henriette Renan, and make two lovers happy.

It is true that Romain Rolland will not let them be happy: Antoinette dies; and Christophe embarks afresh on innumerable adventures. One first of May, in a Socialist riot, his friend, Olivier Jeannin is killed on a barricade; and Christophe, red-handed, is spirited away by his friends, and takes refuge in Switzerland. What an arraignment of the civilisation of Bâle! Give us rather the incoherence of German militarism mixed with German *schwärmerei*! Steep us in the intellectual and social extravagances of France! But keep us free from that death-in-life, the Phariseeism of Bâle! A rigid discipline never relaxed; a collective conscience ever on the watch to punish and deride the faults of individuals; a perpetual constraint in which diversity and spontaneity perish; all the virtues—without the grace of God! And underneath the strict uniformity of its phylacteries, human passions more brutal than elsewhere, because never visited by the open air and sun. As we read the description of Christophe's life in Switzerland, we fall in love with Bohemia. Order is only lovely when it is tempered with grandeur or with grace. But the order of these sordid millionaires is merely a morose economy, a gloomy, dull privation, a lifeless rigour, a sombre constraint. Against this dark background, Romain Rolland projects a figure of almost animal passion.

The story of Jean-Christophe in Switzerland is the history of Wagner and Mathilde Wesendonk. In either case a German musician, fleeing from political difficulties, takes refuge (and takes refuge in Bâle) with a friend who generously comes to his rescue; and in return the musician seduces the wife of his protector.

We know little of the Wesendonks, save that Frau Mathilde was a poetess; I imagine her very different from the wife of Doctor Braun. That kind, fussy little man was oddly mated with the stiff and silent spouse whose large, Michael-Angel-esque type of beauty seemed almost ugly or ridiculous in her awkward provincial clothes. Anna is an uninteresting but perfectly virtuous woman until Jean-Christophe comes to stay in her house. And then music invades her with an incomprehensible passion, turning this sombre young Hausfrau into an imperious Venus.

As she and Christophe sing together the fiery phrases of his Opera, a frenzy overcomes them, and they experience that sort of love in which there is something savage, cosmic, as far as possible removed from our ideas of tenderness or duty. And Christophe, the faithful Christophe, steals from his generous host that little treasure of honour and domestic happiness which was all that Dr Braun had known of life's ideal. Christophe had been received under that roof in his dire necessity, and he betrayed a trust. With a woman whom he barely knew, whom he did not pretend to understand, whom he did not love. Not love? Love was too weak a work to express the torrent of flame that tortured the musician when he thought of

Anna or listened to her voice; and yet he was dimly aware that this fierce instinct, this irresistible intuition, was something less, or more, than human : *Ce n'était pas l'amour, et c'était mille fois plus que l'amour.*

Thus in the Swiss town, in the Calvinist society, which glorified rationalism and made of Intellect the sole motive power of life, Christophe encountered, and was conquered by, that great irreducible Force which makes light of reason and morality, and in front of which all our laws and our scruples and our duties are as idle straws caught in the swirl of a river in flood.

But the strength of that fragility, which is Man, lies in his power of recovery. Like the prodigal son, having fed with the swine, he can always return and go to his Father. Christophe, like Maggie Tulliver in George Eliot's novel, sets duty and faithfulness above passion, and ascends out of the abyss.

'Il comprenait la vanité de son orgueil, la vanité de l'orgueil humain, sous le poing redoutable de la Force qui meut les mondes. Nul n'est maître de soi avec certitude. Il faut veiller. Car si l'on s'endort, la Force se rue en nous et nous emporte . . . dans quels abîmes? Ou le torrent qui nous charrie se retire et nous laisse dans son lit à sec. Il ne suffit même pas de vouloir, pour lutter. Il faut s'humilier devant le Dieu inconnu qui *flat ubi vult*, qui souffle quand il veut, où il veut : l'amour,

la mort ou la vie. La volonté humaine ne peut
rien sans la sienne. Une seconde lui suffit pour
anéantir des années d'efforts. Et, s'il lui plait, il
peut faire surgir l'éternel de la poussière et de la
boue.'

Jean-Christophe sacrifices his delight to his
ideal of conduct. He is rewarded by a great influx
of inspiration. In solitude and renunciation he
takes up his abode on the edge of a mountain, in
the shelter of great woods full of shadow and loneliness; and he lives there in retreat and penitence,
hearing nothing of Anna. And, even as Wagner
in his exile at Venice, when he had renounced
Madame Wesendonk, composed *Tristan und Isolde*,
Jean-Christophe receives at last his inspiration as
a great musician.

The final volume takes us back to Paris, and
thence to Rome. Christophe is now the genius of
his age, but his personal life is still meagre and
sad; no wife, no child, no friend, no love, concen-
trates its elixir in one golden drop. And one day
in the Alps he meets—as a middle-aged woman,
a widow still charming in her tired grace and kind
serenity,—that Countess Berény whom he had
known as a girl in Paris, long ago. And Grazia
Berény incarnates indulgent lazy Italy; as Anna
Braun, Switzerland; as Henriette Jeannin, France;
as the dear, feckless, gentle Sabina, South Germany;
in the long gallery of Christophe's lady-loves.

Of them all, it is Grazia that he desires to marry.

But Grazia, indifferent and gentle, loves Christophe less than her quiet days, her children's interests, her pleasant, nonchalant, and sociable life of a handsome widow 'well left,' who cares above all things for her *quieto vivere*. She is not very interesting, this Grazia, so much in love with peace and measure; she and Christophe would have been as well mated as a sleek and sober Angora with a mastiff ever on the growl (though his bark is worse than his bite), and we are not very sorry when she dies. We have wept so many tears for poor old Louisa (Christophe's mother), for Sabine, for Antoinette, for Olivier, that we have none to spare for the passive and elegant great lady. Neither in the painting of Grazia nor in his image of Rome is our author to be seen at his best. And yet what citizen of Cosmopolis knows Rome as well as Romain Rolland ?

By the end of this tenth volume, Jean-Christophe is no longer young, and all has happened to him that reasonably could be expected to happen. He has mixed in the politics of several nations, he has known fight and flight and exile; he has been poor, he has been famous; he is now the greatest musician of his times. The most exacting reader could not wish to stretch him out much longer on the rack of this tough world. There are ten sizable volumes of him at Mr Ollendorff's—or, if you prefer, seventeen of those wonderful little 'Cahiers de la Quinzaine' (beloved of garrulous and expansive genius) in which M. Charles Péguy has produced

not only M. Romain Rolland, but himself. Now
we know all there is to know, and find that (as in
real life) the climax is middling compared to the
hopes of youth.

Jean-Christophe dies a genius; but we, after
all, have never heard his operas. He dies, like any
other mortal whom a living faith sustains in the
last hour of all. The death of Jean-Christophe
has probably preoccupied more readers than the
end of any other hero in fiction since the great days
of Dickens and Thackeray. We ourselves know
one eminent hand in letters who wrote to the
author suggesting that his hero should disappear
in the wreck of the *Titanic,* conducting the band,
in place of the unforgettable bandmaster. Another
wished him to wander away alone and die in the
desert, after the fashion of Tolstoi.

And I should have liked for him the death of
Péguy—defending his country—leading his men
into battle on the Marne—Ah! there's the rub!
Jean-Christophe was an enemy-alien; he would
have been fighting in the Prussian ranks. For
many years to come M. Rolland's hero cannot be
our hero.

A reader appreciative of the intentions of M.
Rolland might have been sure than Jean-Christophe
would die in no such picturesque or dramatic
fashion, but quietly yield his life on the brink of
a new world, as a wave effaces itself gently and
vanishes in the sand, obliterated by the pressure
of the oncoming wave.

The whole meaning of M. Rolland's book is the continuity of Life, spreading insensibly from soul to soul, from sphere to sphere, in an endless symphony. And the last chapters are full of new characters, pushing forward, rising to maturity; children of the Past in whom the dead revive, fathers of the Future who already are changing the face of our world. The scheme of *Jean-Christophe* (rising thus, and falling, and rising at the end towards the yet unvisioned spectacle of times about to be) recalls the structure of Tolstoi's *War and Peace*.

Jean-Christophe succumbs, sordidly enough, in a Paris lodging, to pneumonia. But he gives up the ghost in a mood of heroic joy, thankful to exchange the worn-out faculties, the dreary, dingy end of life, which are all he can dispose of here, for some undreamed-of harmony and power which await him (as he believes) beyond. Tolstoi himself has not a serener conviction that Life extends illimitably around our tiny sphere, bathing the shores of all the stars in a tide of continual renewal. The unity of the forces which compose a living being must sooner or later dissolve, but the processes of Infinity will reassemble them again. 'Un jour j'e renaîtrai pour de nouveaux combats!' Meanwhile, caught in a rapture beyond the delusion of self, the dying musician feels his personality expand and vanish for a while in something vaster. He is lost in the One-and-All. 'Tu renaîtras . . . Repose. Tout n'est plus qu'un seul cœur.'

And so Jean-Christophe greets a new dawn and leaves behind him, also, on earth a new day. The finest passages of this last volume contain M. Rolland's masterly portrayal of the young France of our times. Surely never was there a generation more unlike its introspective, intellectual forbears: Hamlet has given birth to Harry Hotspur! We must perhaps go back to the times of Ausonius (when the fathers were readers of Seneca and Cicero and the sons hardy Christian barbarians) to find two generations similarly contrasted.

Jean-Christophe was a man of yesterday. His creed was to think no lie, to consent to no injustice, and to love his neighbour as himself. Here M. Rolland shows him in his puissant and solitary decline, dominating a new generation that rises round his knees, strangely different, with other ideals. Truth? Humanity? The old-fashioned words are rarely heard. We hear of Authority, of Order, of the claims of one's race, of the rights and responsibilities of the strong. This new generation, which has witnessed no war, has the mind and disposition of conquerors. Christophe surveys with tender ironical affection the lovable breed of airmen, and sportsmen, and soldiers who fill France to-day—fresh, and frank, and admirably valiant, full of prompt physical courage and intellectual docility.

Jean-Christophe is perhaps the most remarkable work of contemporary fiction: a singular moral fervour, a rare imagination, an unequalled sensibility, a torrent of sarcasm, rancour, revolt, tenderness, stream from its disconcerting pages. But these delicate notations of minute variations in sensibility, though infinitely precious to the psychologist, transgress the limits that strict art prescribes. Romain Rolland sacrifices every grace of measure and composition to his abundance, to his enthusiasm for Life. He has no sense of style. His endless files of short, breathless sentences succeed each other interminably, with no variation, till we experience at last the sensation of a drop falling at regular intervals on the crown of our head ! He has been called 'un volcan qui ne vomit que des cendres.' And then the rare flame strikes out— passages of infinite tenderness or of solemn grandeur.

Still, let me own, while I admire *Jean-Christophe*, I think sometimes with regret of a Turgeneff, no less subtle, who composed his novels at a like tremendous length, and then, pen in hand, went through his manuscript again, and reduced it by two-thirds.

When we open by chance one of those old novels, still famous, long unread, which nourished the minds of our ancestors—*Clarissa Harlowe*, *La Nouvelle Héloise*, or *L'Astrée*, or *Amadis*—or any other of those immense, untidy romances, vast bazaars or stores of their age, which provided several generations with every necessary of life, we are nearly always astonished to find them so interesting and so good. Our forefather's were no fools : what they loved in these books, which were

for them a school of feeling, was not Art, but Life.
Nothing is more instructive in this connection than
to read a letter of Mme de Sévigné's on the interminable masterpiece of La Calprenède; the great
lady, so delicate, so difficile, 'blessée des méchants
styles,' can scarcely understand her own enthusiasm :—

'Le style de La Calprenède est maudit en mille
endroits; de grandes périodes de roman, de méchants
mots—je sens tout cela . . . et cependant je ne
laisse pas de m'y prendre comme à de la glu; la
beauté des sentiments, la violence des passions,
la grandeur des événements tout cela m'entraîne
comme une petite fille.'

And even as Mme de Sévigné was absorbed in
Cléopatre we lose ourselves in *Jean-Christophe*.
Romain Rolland is the great spectator of our times.
Will this quality of moralising criticism, this tendency to preach as well as to paint, and to hold
the mirror up to Nature in a mood of violent irony
—will this gift of satire keep its savour when the
generation whom M. Rolland alternately objurgates
and encourages shall have passed away? It is
difficult to say. He is perhaps one of a race who
exist rather because of a certain flame of life, a
force of personality, than because of the perfection
of their work. Tolstoi, Dr Johnson, Rousseau,
are the great names of this fraternity. *We* are their
characters, they mould *us*, they move *us*, no less

than their puppets.   And we treasure their lessons.
But do we often open *The Rambler* or *La Nouvelle
Héloise*?   Will our children know, as we know,
all the ins and outs of *War and Peace*?   And have
we, finally, the right to include M. Romain Rolland
in this great category of artists who were something more than artists?   It is too soon to say.
We are still lost in the multiplicity of detail, the
immense succession of portraits (not only of persons
but of generations and nations and societies) which
fill the vast canvas of *Jean-Christophe.*

EDMOND ROSTAND

WHEN, in 1886, at eighteen years of age, Edmond Rostand, carried off the Prize for Eloquence at the Academy of Marseilles, the bent of his genius was already plain. For in praising Honoré d'Urfé and his great romance, *Astrée*, the young poet pleaded the cause of a form of art as far removed as possible from the Naturalist formulas which were still the fashion of the hour. And his praise appeared a programme; and the young apologist of Urfé discovered himself to be the apostle of an idealist and sentimental revival.

Despite his amusing originality, and notwithstanding the real nobility of his ideas, Edmond Rostand is not a poet for poets. He was too clever by half—never was a clearer case of the wisdom of the ancients whose proverb ran that 'the half is more than the whole!' His poems are like a brilliant display of fireworks, whose flowers and fusees, whose flashing greens, and blues, and carmines, confuse our sight and prevent our seeing the quiet radiance of the stars behind, above.

And this is not saying that there are no stars in Rostand's poems, no ideas, that is to say, eternally calm and bright. Although not primarily a thinker, yet our poet thinks : there are as many ideas in Rostand as, for instance, in Swinburne.

But too often he uses his unrivalled virtuosity to obscure his plain meaning, as, in some modern music, the importance of the accompaniment drowns the voice. Contrasting the simple nobility of his intention with the quips and the quirks, the puns and the periods, of his rhapsodies, his rhetoric and his rodomontade (the style is catching), shall I say that he reminds us of that mediæval acrobat who, not knowing how to express all his adoration of the Virgin Mary, turned a somersault before her altar? It is amusing to discover that the ideas of Rostand, when we get at them, are not so very different from the ideas of Paul Claudel, who stands at the other extreme of the political and literary horizon.

> 'Ungefähr sagt das der Pfarrer auch,
>   Nur mit ein Bisschen andern Worten.'

Rostand, too, believes that order is rooted in self-sacrifice. His heroes, like Claudel's, strike free of the sterile introspection which marred the art of the Fin-de-Siècle. They make for action, and aim at an end outside themselves (in which they always fail), but Rostand amalgamates his modern Anti-Individualism with the old Liberal romantic, idealist enthusiasm, perfectly sincere so far as it goes. If not devout, he is at least devoted. His plays have generally for their subject some sort of a burnt-offering. For instance in *La Princesse Lointaine*, Bertrand and the Princess sacrifice

their passion to the peace of mind of the dying
Rudel :—

'Oui, les grandes amours travaillent pour le Ciel !'

even as in *Cyrano* the poet renounces his love in
favour of his friend. And that friend again . . .
Cyrano is a veritable vertigo of self-sacrifice !

The tragedy of *L'Aiglon* is the oblation of a
young man's life to a great idea. Chantecler also
is a man—or rather a cock—with a mission to
which he is willing to immolate all personal delight.
The plays of Edmond Rostand are a sort of serum
against selfishness ! Despite their rodomontade
and their buffoonery, they are nobly moral.

But how they irritate a fastidious taste, with
their perpetual posturing, their gesticulations, their
pirouettes, and their impertinence ! Was ever a
real poet and a sincere knight-errant so quaintly
disguised as an acrobat, and sometimes, alas !
even as a commercial 'gent' ! Is it possible to
be at once quite sincere and yet so appallingly
clever? He moves us when he expresses the sense
of patriotism or the praise of courage. He had
a peculiar gift for expressing admiration blent
with pity. He had, in fact, a chivalrous soul,
an instinct for all that is gracious or grand, a
sensibility that was sincere but shallow. Had
he but lived a few months longer, how admirably he would have celebrated the Fêtes of
Victory !

Was he a great poet?   It is perhaps too soon to
say. Bad taste never yet prevented any one from
being a great poet. This is a point on which I
cannot insist too strongly. When Juliet says :—

'Give me my Romeo and when he shall die,
Take him and cut him out in little stars,
And he shall make the face of heaven so fine
That all the world shall be in love with night.'

Shakespeare is writing Rostand with a vengeance.

When in Victor Hugo's *La Forêt Mouillée* the
sparrow makes believe his woodland glade is the
court of Louis XIV., and says in a series of puns,
first of all, to a tuft of heather (bruyère) :—

'Bonjour,
La Bruyère ! (à une branche d'arbre)
Bonjour, Rameau !
(à une corneille sur le rocher)
Bonjour, Corneille !
(au nénufar) Bonjour, Boileau !'

let us admit at once that Victor Hugo wallows
(and not in this instance only) in the very slough
of that bad taste so dear to Rostand. How
pleased Rostand would have been to call the
water-lily, say, John Drinkwater !

But then Shakespeare and Victor Hugo have
amazing qualities wherewith to counter-balance

these conceits. In art, that is everything. The smallest chip of pure gold compensates for a bag full of pebbles : a work of art must be estimated by the degree of its merits and not by the quantity of its defects. If there is dross along with the gold —even though there be much more dross than gold—let us be thankful if the gold itself is pure and unaffected by the presence of the baser residue. There is the question.

I borrow from a book, recently published in French by a Hungarian Professor, M. Haraszti, some details of the youth and origin of Rostand. In 1868, he was born at Marseilles of a wealthy family of merchants and bankers, long established there. For a hundred years, at least, they had all been lovers of the arts. Early in the Nineteenth Century, the quatuors of Beethoven were performed, for the first time in France, in the Rostands' salon. In 1844, a Mademoiselle Victorine Rostand —a great-aunt of the poet's—published a volume of lyrics in the manner of Lamartine. Edmond's uncle, the banker, Alexis Rostand, has composed an opera and more than one oratorio; and his father, the economist Eugène Rostand, is himself a poet. A volume of verse, *Les Sentiers Unis*, published in 1876, celebrates the precocity and charm of the child, Edmond, at that time eight years old; and it is interesting to learn that, even at that early date, he was remarkable for his original grace of words and flow of language :—

'Cette petite langue exquise,
Un vrai jargon de Paradis,
De mots qu'il façonne à sa guise,
De diminutifs inédits;
D'inimitables tours de phrases. . . .'

At eight years of age the child, Edmond Rostand, was certainly the father of the man. As a schoolboy, at the lycée of Marseilles, his Quixotic, pathetic temperament—his characteristic preference for the unsuccessful—was already established. An old, drunken usher scorned by the masters, tormented by the boys, a dreamy Bardolph whom his pupils (on account of his shining nose) surnamed *Pif-Luisant*, was young Rostand's chosen companion. And in his first volume of verse, the poet dedicates a charming poem to the tippler of genius who gave him, perhaps, his first idea of Cyrano :—

'Toi que j'ai tant aimé . .   doux pochard . . . Pif-Luisant.'

At one-and-twenty years of age, Edmond Rostand published his first volume of verse, *Les Musardises*, and shortly afterwards married the beautiful young poetess of *Les Pipeaux*, three years younger than himself. I can remember Rosemonde Gérard in her nineteenth year, a vision of loveliness, as, one evening, in the salon of the old poet, Leconte de Lisle, she stood up, so slender, so smiling, so ravishingly blonde and fresh, and recited a lyric

Photo: Dornac

Edmond Rostand

To face p. 56

as charming as herself. Madame Rostand has a talent of her own, sincere, simple, femininely sentimental. All the lovers in France know her *Chanson éternelle* :—

> 'Car vois-tu chaque jour je t'aime davantage,
> Aujourd'hui plus qu'hier, et bien moins que
>   demain.'

This marriage with Mademoiselle Gérard, grand-daughter of Napoleon's marshal, the victor of Wagram, the victim of Moscow and Waterloo, confirmed Edmond Rostand in his meditations on the dramatic fiasco of the First Empire—that extraordinary antithesis of triumph and disaster, of all tragedies the most touching to martial and patriotic France.

The poet, however, was too wise to undertake this tremendous subject with a 'prentice hand. He made his debut as a playwright in 1894, at the age of twenty-six, with a pretty little fanciful comedy, *Les Romanesques*. A year later, Sarah Bernhardt produced his *Princesse Lointaine*, playing herself the part of the Lady of Tripoli. Sarah Bernhardt again, in the Easter week of 1896, brought out *La Samaritaine*. And at Christmas, 1897, came the conquering hero, *Cyrano de Bergerac*.

I cannot analyse Rostand's plays, which everybody knows, which are (with Kipling's novels) the immense, the international, the universal success of our times ; I cannot calmly plod through the plots of these familiar pieces with the patience I

employ on an obscure play of Paul Claudel's,
known perhaps to a hundred readers in the British
Isles.

Every one (every schoolboy, as Macaulay would
say) has by heart the story of *Cyrano*. We all
remember the chivalrous hero, with his hideous
nose (*Pif-Luisant*), and his romantic nature; his
passion for the pretty blue-stocking, Roxane; his
handsome, stupid friend, Christian, in whom Roxane
thinks she discovers a kindred soul; and how Cyrano
writes Christian's love letters, using the comely
face and figure of his friend as a mask for his own
soul, which thus approaches the beloved, though
under another name; and how Christian, when he
finds that his betrothed really loves, not him, but
the mind of the chivalrous friend whom he has
used as a secretary, gets himself killed in battle,
in order that the two persons whom he loves best
may be free to meet and to mate; and we have not
forgotten that Roxane is inconsolable for the handsome Christian; that Cyrano never has the cruel
courage to reveal his passion until, after fifteen years
of mute misery, he dies : is it not written in the
chronicles of every theatre in Europe?

But it is not this pretty, precious, sentimental
story which made the triumph of *Cyrano*; it is
the indescribable, incommunicable glory and gaiety
of youth, the ardour, the joy, the fun, the fury,
the frolic which make the piece a perfect Fountain
of Jouvence. There is a heroic cheerfulness in
Cyrano, a love of life, a generosity, **an activity, a**

movement, and a flame, which so admirably suit the temper of the dawning Twentieth Century that we hardly know whether the public made the play, or the play the public.

Ten years afterwards, Rostand produced his *L'Aiglon*, which was not greeted with quite the same triumph—the same joy for success, the same rejoicing for victory. But little by little it, too, won its audience; and, personally, I prefer this travesty of Hamlet, with all its faults, to the brilliant, the inimitable *Cyrano*.

For there is a deeper tenderness, a loftier poetry, a more impassioned patriotism in *L'Aiglon* than in any other of Rostand's plays; that superficiality, that haunting sense of insincerity, which elsewhere are as the snake in the grass, are scarcely perceptible here. The poor sick son of the dead hero, the 'ineffectual angel,' the sensitive, inefficient young Duc de Reichstadt, Napoleon's heir, is drawn with a feeling and a depth of knowledge which make me suspect that in his sad protagonist the poet drew, not merely a historical personage, but his own generation, the children of 1870, the sons of the defeat, decadent and dilettante, incapable of action, but so touching and so often noble in their disinterestedness, their sense of the Ideal, their love of liberty. Rostand, I think, in love and pity has drawn their portrait—and then drew that of Flambeau to inspire a bolder generation.

The boldest of the bold is Chantecler, the cock of Gaul. In his legend of Chantecler, Edmond

'Rostand bids us mark that courage needs more to its making than mere temerity. He does not say, with Danton, 'De l'audace, de l'audace, et toujours de l'audace.' He says, 'De l'audace, et puis du bon sens, et puis le sens de la vérité!'

This history of a poultry-yard has somewhat disconcerted the adorers of *Cyrano*. But Boileau and the big-wigs of the Court of Louis Quatorze were doubtful at first (and thought that Pegasus had taken to pedestrian by-ways) when La Fontaine produced his inimitable *Fables*; and only a few years ago in London the public, expectant of more *Plain Tales from the Hills*, gave a hesitating reception to that *Jungle Book* of Mr Kipling's which already (in France at least) is regarded as his principal title to honour. There are always amateurs who insist on repetition, and blame Wouvermans if he paint a picture without a white horse in it. To my thinking, Edmond Rostand proved himself a poet in looking no further than the farm-yard gate to find a subject for his verse.

There is something singularly impressive to the dreamer, to the man of imagination, in the certainty that our world is inhabited by a race of beings who see the things we see, and move in the circles wherein we have our being, but look on everything from a different point of view, and perhaps with different senses. Ants, that have no ears, yet hear through their feet, perceiving the vibrations conveyed by solid bodies; flies, whose innumerable eyes discern the X-rays as a colour;

these, and homing swallows, are more mysterious
than fairies. In the eye of a mystic, a cock is no
less wonderful than a ghost; a mouse than a muse;
a primrose by the river's brim than the herb moly
(that white-blossomed flower which Hermes gave
to Ulysses), or than the plant called Love-in-
Idleness that charmed Titania's eyes. The fact
that so immense a variety of existences shares with
us the boon of life, and feels the same sun, is a
perpetual fable to a certain order of minds, who
may affirm with Chantecler :—

'Et quant à moi, Madame, il y a bien longtemps
Qu' un râteau dans un coin, une fleur dans un vase,
M'ont fait tomber dans une inguérissable extase,
Et que j'ai contracté devant un liseron
Cet émerveillement dont mon œil reste rond !'

This was Rostand's attitude during the first two
acts, the two acts in which he showed himself a
poet. There is a humour, a tenderness, a charm
which recall Hans Andersen's inimitable stories in
his vision of a world where none of our thoughts,
none of our knowledge, but perhaps most of our
feelings have free play. Man is absent.

'Malebranche dirait qu'il n'y a plus une âme;
Nous pensons humblement qu'il reste encore
    des cœurs.'

The Cock's Hymn to the Sun is so devoid of all
our cosmic ideas that I have heard more than one

critic deride it on this account; but how wise, how
truly a seer, is the poet in showing the wonder of
the sun as it appears to an animal who sees no
further than the almond trees at the end of the
valley! The Infinite is the Infinite, though we
look at it through a keyhole, and to an animal or
an infant the sun is still the sun. The poet has
chosen just those aspects and effects which may
appeal to a mind deprived of reason no less than
to ourselves. The sun dries the dew from the grass,
and lends a grace even to the faded almond flowers;
the sun shining on a pane of glass or the soapy
water in a tub makes of them a glory; the sun
turns the sunflower westward in his course, and
makes the tin cock on the church tower a dazzling
chanticleer; the sun shining through the boughs
of the lime-walk sheds on the gravel trembling pools
of light which wobble so lovely that one scarcely
dares to walk there; the sun makes a banner of the
clout that dries on the hedge; and gilds with a wonderful lustre the varnished earthenware crock in the
farm-yard; thanks to the sun the hayrick has gold
on his hat and the hive has gold on her hood :—

'Gloire à toi sur les prés! Gloire à toi dans les
    vignes!
Sois béni parmi l'herbe et contre les portails!
Dans les yeux des lézards et sur l'aile des
    cygnes!
        O toi qui fais les grandes lignes
        Et qui fais les petits détails!

'C'est toi qui, découpant la sœur jumelle et
　　sombre
Qui se couche et s'allonge au pied de ce qui luit,
De tout ce qui nous charme as tu doubler le
　　nombre,
　　　À chaque objet donnant une ombre
　　　Souvent plus charmante qui lui !

' Je t'adore, Soleil ! Tu mets dans l'air des roses,
Des flammes dans la source, un dieu dans le
　　buisson !
Tu prends un arbre obscur et tu l'apothéoses !
　　　O Soleil ! toi sans qui les choses
　　　Ne seraient que ce qu'elles sont !'

In this beautiful ode, Edmond Rostand really
enriched French literature with an image of the
greatest thing in the universe as it may appear to
the humblest living being; and, despite here and
there an ugly, trivial turn of phrase (we shudder at
tu l'apothéoses), despite the hard, happy-go-lucky lilt
of the verse, its simplicity is full of a natural magic.

No less than man, just as naturally, and (owing
to his more limited imagination) even more fer-
vently, Chantecler considers himself the centre of
the universe. In a recent letter to Jean Coquelin
about the scene-painting and staging of his play
Rostand has put his point of view :—

' L'idée de mon décor est ceci : donner la sensation qu'une petite allée de jardin est, pour les
volailles, une voie immense, une Via Appia.'

They live no less than us in the middle of immen-
sities, only, from their lower standpoint, they
remark (even less than we do) the disproportion
between the world they inhabit, and the unthinkable Infinity they leave unmodified.

'Très peu de ciel dans ce décor; c'est important
de donner l'impression qu'étant très bas, à hauteur
de poule, on en voit moins.'

Knowing so little about it, Chantecler is convinced that the magic of his cock-a-doodle-doo!
makes the sun rise every morning! The pearl of
the poem is the scene in the second act, where
Chantecler confides this marvellous secret to the
gloriosa donna della sua mente, the Hen-Pheasant,
who has taken refuge in the poultry-yard. A
pheasant sees more of the world than a cock, flies
and rockets up in the sky, dwells in the forest, and
therefore, half-sceptical, half-scandalised, she listens
while Chantecler, manlike, expatiates on the necessity of his existence.

So far at least the myth is charming in its quaint
philosophy, the characters appear full of humour
each of them as French as French can be; for
why should not animals as well as human beings,
have a nationality and racial qualities of their
own? Chantecler is a coxcombed Don Quixote,
chimerical, infatuate, peremptory, and brave; but
he is, we have said, a *French* Don Quixote, and so
he represents not only chivalry, but also order and

authority; he is not only generous but masterful; loyal to his subordinates, vain of his beauty and prone to vaunt it; and he thinks himself the natural sultan of every female fowl. Chantecler, like Don Quixote, is absurd; and yet not merely lovable, but honourable in his absurdity. If his adventure proves anything, it is that an illusion and a chimera are necessary to prevent us from lapsing into scepticism or savagery.

Chantecler, with his valiance, his vain-glory, and his optimism, is one type of French character (a noble or military sort of type); another French fowl is the blackbird, the 'Merle.' Le Merle is a French Mephistopheles—a *Geist der stets verneinet* —paralysing all effort by his scepticism, his criticism, his pitiless raillery, his pitiable *blague*, which is often merely,—

> 'Une prudence, un art de rester vague,
> Un élégant moyen de n'avoir pas d'avis.'

He is

> 'Le petit croque-mort de la Foi.'

The blackbird is at once a *boulevardier* and an *intellectuel*. He is the 'Chat Noir,' he is Montmartre; alas, he is the pretext for many bad verses, execrable conceits, and parlous puns. Not that a poet, I repeat, is obliged to have good taste; but there are moments when the pun kills the poem. When the Blackbird says to the philosophic

fowl, 'Fichez le Kant !' (camp); when he interrupts,
'C'est vieux œufs !' (vieux jeu)—surely he out-
distances the most trivial dialogues of Moth and
Armado; and we answer with old Chaucer,—

> 'Allas ! conceytes stronge !'

and exclaim with Shakespeare's Troilus,—

> 'He would pun thee unto shivers !'

Chantecler took seven years in the writing. I
know nothing of the mystery of its composition;
but one may perhaps suppose that Rostand
wrote the first two acts in a real objective vein
of poetry—tender, amused, imaginative, and then
shut them in a drawer, forgot them, and some time
later on, resumed the task in a mood of intellectual
exasperation against the literary world of Paris.
In this latter part, the poultry-yard à la La Fontaine
has changed to a parody of the boulevard and all
the charm has vanished. This third act is a sort
of bantam imitation of *Jean-Christophe*, in *La Foire
Sur la Place*. There is an operatic beauty in the
hymn of the owls; there is gaiety and good humour
later on; and, in the episode of the Nightingale,
I find a tender philosophic loveliness. And yet
we cannot defend ourselves from the impression
that Rostand wrote the first two acts in a sudden
vein of poetry; and then, long afterwards, took
up the incompleted masterpiece and finished it as
best he could, with the help of his gifted family

circle. We know that of the four Rostands, three were poets—Edmond Rostand, his wife, and Maurice, their elder son. . . . This, of course, is the mere supposition of a critic's idle brain.

We might take for the motto of all Rostand's work, a saying of Friar Trophime in *La Princesse Lointaine :* 'La seule vertu, c'est l'enthousiasme.' Like Maurice Barrès, Rostand too, in his way, was a Professor of Energy. In his last years, he was writing a new *Faust*. That story of a great Intellectualist who quits the kingdom of his mind for the freshest fields and humblest pastures of the realm of instinct is well suited to the genius of Edmond Rostand. Why should he not write a new *Faust*? Did not the classic poets of antiquity all work on the same subjects? And did not Corneille and Racine (in the same year, if I remember right) each of them produce a *Titus et Bérénice*? It would be interesting to read the *Faust* of Rostand's eager imagination. (Edmond Rostand, as I have said, is not a poet for poets. He had the same sort of reputation in France that Mr Kipling has in England—colossal, undoubtedly, but hardly literary.) Either of them, perhaps, is more appreciated in Europe at large—in Europe and America—than in the salons of their own metropolis. Something inelegant, cocksure, aggressive, sometimes a little superficial, checks in either of them the natural homage of the difficult—of the delicate. They gather no violets—Athena's, Sappho's violets !—but what a quantity of buttercups and daisies !

PAUL CLAUDEL

It is not easy to account for the enthusiasm aroused in France, among the younger writers, by the works of Paul Claudel, unless we accept the explanation that, with all his faults, he is a great poet. He is a difficult author, often wilfully obscure and allusive; his dramas are lyrical symbols rather than plays and, whatever he write, ode or tragedy, he uses the same medium, a sort of rhythmical prose, sometimes like Walt Whitman's dithyrambs, and sometimes like the Psalms.

Nothing is less familiar, less lifelike, more hieratic, than the manner of Claudel. In every detail of his art he innovates and experiments : style, language, conception, even the very names of his characters bear witness to a restless personality, starting off on a quest of his own, continuing no other writer, impatient of yoke or path. And though he lose himself and stumble in his search for an Ideal, be sure he will never turn back, never take the highroad, but just go on persistently, making a rule and a guide for himself out of the exigencies of his own peculiar temperament and creating a doctrine out of his fantasies.

He is often absurd, violent, rhetorical, extravagant; his plays are frequently no more than psychological dialogues between the dissociated

elements of his own personality. At other times
he will suggest to us a Pindar disguised in the
mantle of Saint Thomas Aquinas. He is often as
unreal as Il Greco! And yet this incomplete and
exasperating poet is, in truth, a great artist (or
at least has the makings of one), and it is not out
of pure perversity that a Francis Jammes has
compared him to Pascal, that others have called
him *haut comme Dante*. They exaggerate; but
there is in them more understanding than in the
perplexed spectator of *L'Échange* or *L'Otage*, who
is persuaded that M. Claudel only does it to annoy.

What is then the message that Paul Claudel is
obscurely crying to his generation, faltering like
the prophet, 'â, â, Domine, nescio loqui?'

He brings to these young men, accustomed to
the shifting relativities of Bergson, bathed since
their boyhood in the perpetual flow of a stream
whose onrush falls into no estuary, the vision of
an absolute Unity. To Claudel, movement, life,
are but a transient wave-and-wobble on the surface
of Reality, 'un tremblement essentiel devant la
face du Saint.' Behind the streaming veil he
discerns the Eternal Face within, ever serenely
smiling. Behind Life there is that which Life is
not : there is the living God. Hidden by the
mists of our apparent disorder, he divines a crystal
sphere—an indivisible, unalterable, absolute Existence—where right is always right, where wrong is
always wrong, to all eternity. This religious
idealism brings a sense of rest and peace to minds

unconsciously fatigued by Bergson's theories of incessant evolution. And then, also, the principle of perpetual change is a solvent of energy; Faith is a school of energy; and energy is what France chiefly prizes among her many spiritual gifts :—

'Tournons donc, comme la religieuse Chaldée, nos yeux vers le ciel absolu où les astres, en un inextricable chiffre, ont dressé notre acte de naissance et tiennent greffe de nos pactes et de nos serments.' (*Connaissance du Temps*, p. 40.)

It is the prose writings and the Odes of Paul Claudel that give us a clue to the secret of his influence, but it is his plays that have made his reputation. Strange and dithyrambic as is their form, complicated and obscure as is their substance, they are the same in *Tête d'Or*, composed in 1889 (when the poet was one-and-twenty years of age), and in *L'Annonce Faite à Marie*, played in Paris in 1912, of which a definitive version was published in 1914. The same carnal and violent imagination, the same heroic romance, are set to serve the same central theme : the insufficiency of worldly success.

It is a commonplace to say that the Twentieth Century is an age of deeds, not words, that the young generation (in France especially) are born not dreamers, but doers. Claudel himself is a traveller and a man of action. A native of Picardy (he was born in 1868 of a Vosgian stock,) he has

lived of late years little in Paris and in the world
of letters. A pupil of the Symbolists, Arthur Rimbaud
and Mallarmé, he left France for America in his
early youth, at four-and-twenty years of age, to
nake his way in the Consular service. It would
ɔe interesting to learn in what degree this aristocrat
(by temperament at least), this Catholic, suffered
the contact of the democratic prophet, Walt Whitman. There are points of similarity, not only in
the form. A few years later we find him Consul at
Tien-Tsin (one of the finest of his odes is dated
from Pekin), and since then, Paul Claudel has become
an authority and a specialist in the Chinese affairs
of the French Foreign Office. In 1908 he returned
to Europe in order to assume the duties of Consul
at Prague, then at Frankfort-on-the-Main, and,
at the present moment, he is Consul-General at
Rio-Janeiro.

The poet, therefore, is no idle singer of an empty
day; and his heroes, too, are men of action—a
general in *Tête d'Or*; a hydraulic engineer in *La
Jeune Fille Violaine* ; an American merchant in
L'Échange; a Consul in *Partage de Midi*; a political
agitator in *L'Otage*; an architect in *L'Annonce
Faite à Marie*. And the sense of his plays, if we
read them right, is that not poetic feeling, but
effort, should be our daily bread; that mere sentiment is sterile and incoherent (the adventurous
Louis Laine in *L'Échange* is the slave of the
sentiment of the hour); that activity, even when
it is evil activity, may bring forth a better future

(the murderous Mara in *L'Annonce,* the brutal
Toussaint in *L'Otage* are, no less, the begetters of
to-morrow); but that while energy should inspire
our life, yet none the less there is something
infinitely better which comes not by taking pains,
something better than all our work and labour,
just as there is something infinitely better than
Life, which may descend upon us, uplift us, carry
us into a superior sphere : there is the Grace of
God, there is Inspiration, there is 'La Muse qui
est la Grâce !'

For, at heart, this poet of airmen and soldiers
is a sort of lay monk, reserving his palm of praise,
not for the conqueror, but for the rapt ecstatic—
the solitary, dying with half his labours unachieved,
the hermit Violaine, the broken-hearted wife of
Toussaint Turelure.   And we might inscribe all
his books, for an epigraph, with that line of the
Vulgate, which Renan wrote in the monks' ledger
at Monte Cassino : 'Unum est necessarium . . .
et Maria elegit optimam partem.'

From these plays—romantic, disconcerting, over-
subtle—emerge (as Meredith's women, wonderfully
human, break through the tinsel veil of his arti-
ficialities) the most living and the most lovable
of heroines.   The Marthe of *L'Échange* may be a
symbol, may mean the Church, as we have been
told, or (as the poet himself has recently informed
us) may incarnate one state of his own soul; she
is certainly the most adorable of Frenchwomen—
French and woman to the tips of her fingers,

prudent and pure, silent and sage, wife-like and wise, full of well-planned economies and exquisite order :— a type our poet is never weary of reproducing.

The heroine of *L'Otage* might be her sister; the long, slim, silent, energetic girl, who is all conscience and courage, lifted just one degree higher; no heroine, no virgin merely, but a saint, stretched on the Cross to the extreme of human greatness. The one exception in M. Claudel's gallery is the extraordinarily living portrait of an Englishwoman, or Irishwoman, in *Partage de Midi* : Ysé, with her fresh beauty and her yellow hair—Ysé, who is just woman, as Eve was woman; all passion, instinct, sex, all beauty, flower and grace : Ysé, whom we associate mysteriously with the Epode of *La Muse qui est la Grâce*, when the poet, overcome by memory, cries to the Grace of God :—

'Va-t-en ! Je me retourne désespérément vers
    la terre !
Va-t-en ! Tu ne m'ôteras pas ce froid goût
    de la terre,
Cette obstination avec la terre qu'il y a dans
    la moelle de mes os et dans le caillou de
    ma substance, et dans le noir noyau de
    mes viscères !

   .   .   .   .   .   .

'Qui a crié? J'entends un cri dans la nuit
    profonde !
J'entends mon antique sœur des ténèbres qui
    remonte une autre fois vers moi,

L'épouse nocturne qui revient une autre fois
  vers moi, sans mot dire,
Une autre fois vers moi, avec son cœur, comme
  un repas qu'on se partage dans les ténèbres,
Son cœur, comme un pain de douleur, et comme
  un vase plein de larmes.'

It is extraordinary that this great prose-poet, who is known at least to an *élite* in Italy, who, in the course of the year 1913, has been acted with success in Germany, at Strasburg, at Frankfort, and at Dresden; whose plays, in 1914, have twice excited enthusiasm on the Parisian stage, should have no public in our islands. Is there no translator brave enough to undertake *L'Otage*, the most accessible of Claudel's plays, or *L'Annonce*, so like the poems of our own pre-Raphaelites? The readers who enjoy Thomas Hardy's *Dynasts*, or Doughty's plays of Britain, should not find them impossibly difficult, they might even welcome the fresh source of a singularly noble pleasure.

In order to encourage and enlighten this hypothetical translator, I will run through the plots of the principal of these dramas. It is not an easy task, for no sooner has Claudel accustomed his readers to a set of characters, than he is out with a second version of the same play; and lo! in the twinkling of an eye, all is changed. I do not advise my imaginary translator to begin with the first of these pieces, *Tête d'Or*, which is really intolerably prolix. Yet there is much that is fine and moving

in the sombre, magnificent pictures which show
us the folly of individualism. The hero staggers
on the stage, like Lear burdened with the dead
body of Cordelia, carrying the corpse of his young
wife; he is young and strong, but he has not been
able to save her; and under the beating rain in the
open field, he digs her grave and lays her there :—

'Va là, entre dans la terre crue ! A même ! Là
où tu n'entends plus et ne vois plus, la bouche
contre le sol.
'Comme quand, sur le ventre, empoignant les
oreillers, nous nous ruons vers le sommeil !
'Et maintenant je te chargerai une charge de
terre sur le dos !'

Simon is the man of action, the strong man, the
soldier. He becomes a popular general, a sort of
Bonaparte, whom his soldiers on account of his
touzled yellow curls call Goldilocks : Tête d'Or.
And, in the second act, he returns from a brilliant
victory having redeemed his country. But he
finds his one friend dying. This poor lad implores
the hero to save him—or, at least, to console him.
And Goldilocks discovers the limits of his power !
Finally he himself, though a king triumphant,
perishes as miserably.

'Que je grandisse dans mon unité,' cried Goldilocks. But one man alone, however great, is little;
and his last words are : 'Je n'ai été rien.'

This play was written by the unregenerate
Claudel; it shows a nature born to mysticism and
religion, with as yet no active faith. A few years
later, we find our poet the most convinced of
Catholics. Like the poet, Cœuvre (in his play,
La Ville), we leave him, at the end of the second
act, a simple dilettante; and when next the curtain
rises we find him resplendent in priestly vestments.
Not that Claudel has ever actually taken orders,
yet in his own way he is a priest and ordained to
a ministry. He, too, has found in thought a second
birth—'dans la profondeur de l'étude, une second
naissance.'

And now he writes to promulgate his certitude.
Man does not live for man but for God; the happiness of self is an illusion; the soul alone exists;
the only true order is based on sacrifice and associa-
tion : such is the lesson that all his plays expound.

La Jeune Fille Violaine is an early study for
Claudel's masterpiece, *L'Annonce faite à Marie*.
It is a modern play, a touching, romantic story,
not unlike the work of the modern Irish school.
The setting is a large farm near Soissons. The
heroine, Violaine, is the elder of the two daughters
of the house. Because she is so happy and he so
miserable, the young girl bestows an innocent kiss
on Pierre de Craon, the hydraulic engineer, who
loves her and whom she cannot love; she embraces
him 'en tout bien et tout honneur;' but, just as
her fresh lips are on her lover's cheek her jealous
younger sister, Mara, opens the door and stealthily

witnesses their farewell; and Mara thinks that her sister is the man's mistress.

Their father, Anne Vercors, the master of the farm, is forced to leave his home for America, where his brother has died, to go to the relief of two young nephews. Before setting out on so long a journey, he wishes to marry one of his daughters to a young neighbour, Jacques Hury, an active and honourable man, capable of managing the land. Violaine is the eldest; Violaine shall be the bride, and, having celebrated their betrothal, the farmer sets out consoled.

Violaine loves her promised husband. Alas, the treacherous Mara loves him too! She tells Jacques of her sister's kiss, and suggests that Violaine's love is given to Pierre de Craon. She confides her own desperate passion to her mother —vows she will hang herself in the woodshed on the wedding-day.

'Tell Violaine,' she says, 'tell Violaine.'

And Violaine gives up her hope of happiness in order to save her sister.

Mara is not yet satisfied : Mara the practical, Mara the unanswerable,—

'You cannot stay here *now*,' she says to the sad Violaine. 'And I suppose you will hardly again think of marrying? Every one knew you were betrothed to Jacques.'

'No,' says Violaine, 'I do not think of marrying.

'Then, in that case, you may as well give me

your half of the farm! What use would it be to
you, if you do not live with us, and if you do not
marry? Come, sign! Here is the pen!'

And then, while Violaine signs away her birth-
right, Mara seeks in the hearth a handful of wood
ashes to pounce the signature, and having dried
the writing, flings the remainder of the hot, stifling
dust in her sister's face. And she laughs, coarse
and gay; but the ashes set up an inflammation
that ends by blinding Violaine for life.
When the third act begins, several years have
passed. Violaine, an outcast and a beggar, a sort
of pious wise-woman, lives alone in a wood. The
peasants revere her as a saint, and indeed her
virtues are acceptable in the sight of Heaven, so
that she performs many miracles. (This situation
in a modern play appears less far-fetched than it
would in England among the fields of France,
where the wise-woman and the sorcerer, the 'meije'
and the 'rebouteux' and the 'jetteuse de sorts,'
with their herbs and their charms and their clever
massage, still play so large a part in the life of the
remoter villages.) The art of Violaine is much
esteemed by the simple rustics that know neither
her name nor her birthplace. And so one day, in
order to consult the wise woman of the wood,
Mara sets out with her first-born, blind from birth.
She knows not whom she goes out in the wilderness
to see, as she joins company with a poor woman
bent on the same quest. They track the healer

for some while vainly, through a wood, in the
snow :—

La Femme : Si c'est pas un malheur de courir
les bois comme ça à mon âge ! Pour sûr que ça
me fera pas de bien !

Mara : Alors on ne sait pas où elle gîte?

La Femme : Un jour ici, l'autre ailleurs. Et
puis des mois sans qu'on la voie. Faut la traquer
comme une bête.

Et comme ça, votre petit est aveugle?

Mara : Oui.

La Femme : Moi, j'ai mal dans le corps.
(*Silence. Il neige.*)

   .   .   .   .   .   .

Mara : Alors c'est des miracles qu'elle fait?

La Femme : Y a pas de miracles, que vous êtes
simple ! C'est ce qu'on appelle la 'force,' voilà !

Y a pas de miracles. C'est seulement la 'force'
vous comprenez? On m'a bien expliqué tout ça.

At last Mara finds the wise woman in a cavern,
and blind Violaine gives to her sister's child the
gift of sight.

The fourth act brings us back to the farm.
Mara, incurably jealous, has murdered Violaine,
and left her for dead in a ditch. But Pierre de
Craon has found her body, and brings her back to
her old home, still breathing, though blind and
bleeding. Jacques Hury opens to them and sees,
all mangled, murdered, the broken form of the

woman whose fresh youth he had loved. Violaine
tells him all. She dies forgiving, reconciling, everybody—even the murderous Mara who, in her dreadful, jealous, earthly way, had after all 'loved much.'
Mara, not Violaine, was the mother of the child !
And we divine that Mara is Profane Love, and
Violaine that other Love.

'L'Amor che muove il sole e l'altre stelle.'

Quite recently, in 1912, Paul Claudel has made
the symbol clearer in a new version of his play
The Angelus (*L'Annonce faite à Marie*), though it
is at some expense of the fresh, primitive grace,
the Celtic charm of the earlier conception. There
is something artificial, stiff, consciously pre-Raphael-
ite in *L'Annonce faite à Marie*, but also a rare
spiritual beauty.

In the second version, place and personages
remain unchanged, but the time is altered; we
are no longer modern but plunged in the early
Middle Ages. Anne Vercors, the master of the
farm, leaves his home not on an errand of charity
to America, but in order to join the Crusade.
Pierre de Craon, instead of canalising rivers, builds
cathedrals : he is a great master-mason, so gifted
that, by a special dispensation he is allowed at
large, although a secret leper. And Violaine's
kiss of compassion infects her with his disease.

This seems to me a grave artistic error, since
to some extent it exculpates the faithless Jacques,

the cruel Mara, who follow but the fashion of their age in driving a leper from her home. But the end : the death of Violaine, stifled under a cart-load of sand, from which the treacherous Mara has drawn the back panel; and the return of Anne Vercors; and the relative repentance of the obstinate Mara; and the great mystical wind that rises and uplifts us into a region where happiness and tragedy are lost in a peace beyond understanding—all this moves us deeply in the second rendering.

Each version has its beauties, and either makes us realise the Celtic base of France—at least, of the north of France. The French have ever Rome upon their lips, and their education has been strictly Latin since the time of the Gallo-Romans, but, by instinct and blood, they are Celts : no deep racial difference divides a Paul Claudel from a Synge, or a Barbey d'Aurevilly from a Walter Scott.

La Jeune fille Violaine presents no great diffi-culties to a reader broken in by a sufficient course of recent Irish literature. *L'Échange* is simpler still—one of the most spontaneous and agreeable, as also one of the earliest of Claudel's pieces. It is a little tragedy with four personages : Louis Laine, an adventurer, a libertine, a man incapable of discipline or of order—in fact, an Individualist, and, as such, abominable in the sight of Paul Claudel; his wife, the pure girl he has eloped with, a Frenchwoman of a type which Claudel is never weary of reproducing. Laine, an American, has carried off his French bride to the New World, a land whose traditions and conditions are contrary to all her experience. Louis Laine incarnates the mercantile American spirit, but he knows nothing of its energy, its initiative; qualities swiftly apprehended by the self-possessed and diligent Marthe. She says to the Yankee, Laine's employer, Thomas Pollock Nageoire (Finn) :—

'Thomas Pollock, il y a plusieurs choses que j'aime en vous.

'La première c'est que, croyant qu'une chose est bonne, vous ne doutez pas de faire tous vos efforts pour l'avoir.

'La seconde, comme vous le dites, c'est que vous connaissez la valeur des choses, selon qu'elles valent plus ou moins.

'Vous ne vous payez point de rêves, et vous ne vous contentez point d'apparences, et votre commerce est avec les choses réelles.

'Et par vous toute chose bonne ne demeure point inutile.

'Vous êtes hardi, actif, patient, rusé, opportun, persévérant; vous êtes calme, vous êtes prudent, et vous tenez un compte exact de tout ce que vous faîtes. Et vous ne vous fiez point en vous seul.

'Mais vous faîtes ce que vous pouvez, car vous ne disposez point des circonstances.

'Et vous êtes raisonnable, et vous savez soumettre votre désir, votre raison aussi.

'Et c'est pourquoi vous êtes grand et riche.'

Thomas Pollock is the natural mate of Marthe;
and he judges her ill-matched with her vagabond
adventurer of a husband so much better suited
to his own feckless mate, the dissolute actress,
Letchy Elbernon. So he proposes an exchange.
He will divorce anew (he is familiar with the process)
and marry Marthe, endowing sufficiently Letchy
to make it worth Laine's while to espouse her.
Ah, if Nature were all ! But to the delicate Marthe,
marriage is a sacrament, and only in marriage
may she love entirely anything less than God.
Unconsecrated love is but an 'abjuration passionnée'
—'la seule vie qu'on puisse partager—le seul
échange possible—c'est le marriage,' as we have
learned already in *Partage de Midi.*
So Thomas Pollock argues in vain :—

'Où est le règle de la vie
Si un homme ancien et éprouvé,
Mûr, solide, avisé, capable, réfléchi, ne cherche
    pas
A avoir une chose qu'il trouve bonne?
Et si je suis plus riche et plus sage que lui,
    est-ce ma faute?
J'ai été honnête avec lui . . .
Je lui ai offert de l'argent et il est tombé
    d'accord avec moi.'

When the mad and vicious Letchy has murdered
Laine and ruined her husband, Marthe still stands
firm. Her love is with the dead adventurer; his

duty is to the gibbering Letchy. They two can pretend but to a perfect friendship. They stand there loveless, homeless, penniless, but there is in either an innate capacity which dreads no change of circumstance. The fortunes of the American will rise from the ashes like the Phœnix; and Marthe fears nothing, having that to offer which is always needed :—

'I can earn my living by my needle—just finish the piece of sewing that lies across my knee.'

Here, despite the lyric disorder of our poet's style, we have a fable perfectly clear, and four personages quite alive and characteristic. Yet Paul Claudel has set before us not a story, but a symbol.

As he explained in a recent letter to the *Figaro*, his personages mean more than meets the eye. Aware of the symbolism of our poet, mindful that he is essentially a pupil of Mallarmé, a subtle critic has already interpreted *L'Échange*: Marthe was the Catholic Church; Laine, her seducer, was the Romantic spirit; Thomas Pollock, the friend to whom in her distress she reaches her hand, was to stand for the spirit of social activity. Nothing could be neater than this gloss, so admirably typical of our times; and I think, for my part, that Paul Claudel would have been wise to leave his ingenious scholiast in possession of his commentary.

When a poet is so obscure that he needs a Browning Society or a Dante Society, or a Claudel clique, to discover his meaning, he should never turn on his interpreters, pointing-pole in hand; it is not playing the game. They have found out something—perhaps better than what he originally meant. M. Claudel, however, informs us of his real intention.

L'Échange was written in 1893 and 1894, at New York and Boston, where the young poet was occupied in the Consular service, and this melodrama is in reality a lyric, an expression of his own feelings during those first years of administrative exile :—

'I realised at last those old dreams of flight and travel to which my hero, Louis Laine, gives expression; and yet my heart was full of homesickness, of the sense of strangeness, of not belonging to my surroundings : my second personage, Marthe, expresses this regret of my native land. . . . From another point of view, the play, which is the drama of exile, is also that of a young man, a poet, obliged to choose between two vocations, apparently contradictory : on the one hand, free love, independent life, unfettered fancy, art; on the other hand, the obstinate, divine, conservative forces : conscience, family, religion, the Church, and a man's sworn faith.'

But these symbolic forms of art should enjoy

the **divine** liberty of music. Like Calverley's
lyric 'the meaning is what you please'; or as
Claudel himself puts it :—

'L'intérêt d'un drame doit dépasser l'anecdote
qu'il raconte; il veut dire quelquechose; quelquechose de général et qui n'est étranger à aucun
des spectateurs.'

All Claudel's dramas are symbols; all of them
tend to the condition of music; and yet all of them
are profoundly impregnate with his individual
experience. They take place all over the globe,
because Claudel, a pupil of the School of Political
Sciences, has followed the consular career in many
climates. He has visited India, Japan. He has
spent years of his life in China, in Bohemia, at
Frankfort, in Switzerland. He is almost as great
a traveller as Loti. But the multiplicity of experience, the knowledge of many men and many ways
of life, which in Loti's case has increased an innate
tendency to scepticism—deepening it to an intellectual nihilism— has sent Claudel off at a tangent
back to the unquestioned certitudes of his childhood's
prayers : he dare not be less than the devoutest
Catholic, for that way madness lies. Faith with
him is an appetite, almost a carnal satisfaction.
   The theme of *L'Échange*—the incompatibility
of Action and the Soul—is the subject of one of
the most intense and original of Claudel's plays,
Partage de Midi, a play revered and cherished by

the poet's esoteric admirers partly, no doubt, on its own considerable merits, but also because it is not to be bought. (It was published in an edition of a hundred and fifty copies for the benefit of a chosen few, admitted to this record of a private experience, so enveloped in symbolism that, of those hundred and fifty, perhaps, not fifteen could lift the veil.)

Here again four personages fill the stage : Ysé, who is just woman, as Eve was woman, all passion, instinct, sex, all beauty, freshness, grace, as devoid of a spiritual soul as any houri; her husband, De Ciz, a gentle, inefficient man of pottering mediocrity ; Amalric, the man of action, the adventurer, the Empire-builder, the colonial à la Kipling; and Mesa, the mystic, the virgin, the visionary, the man for whom there is but one thing needful. And all these men belong to Ysé in turn.

The theme is double : first, the gradual conquest of Parseval by Kundry—of the imaginative and spiritual man by the instinctive woman. Neither has grasped the secret of love, but Ysé at least apprehends it :—

Ysé: L'amour même? . . . Ça, je ne sais ce que c'est.

Mesa : Eh bien, ni moi non plus . . . Cependant, je puis comprendre.

Ysé: Il ne faut pas comprendre, mon pauvre Monsieur !

Il faut perdre connaissance !

And for the full space of a year Mesa loses, in the arms of Ysé, that consciousness of a fuller life, hidden behind the tattered screen of appearances, which had long been to him the *Unum necessarium*.

But Mesa has his revenge. We make acquaintance with these four persons on a ship sailing eastwards, just as they cross the line. De Ciz is an errant engineer, in search of employment; Amalric is a trader ruined yesterday, but sure of his million to-morrow; Mesa is, by his worldly situation, a sort of Sir Robert Hart, a great functionary, equally indispensable to the Europeans and the Chinese, but by temperament he is a mystic, meditating the full oblation, hesitating whether or no he shall embrace the life of a monk. Ysé is a new world to the visionary Mesa :—

'Il fait bon près d'une femme !
On est comme assis à l'ombre et j'aime à
  l'entendre parler avec une grande sagesse,
Et me dire des choses dures, malignes,
Pratiques, bassement vraies, comme les femmes
  savent en trouver. Cela me fait du bien.'

The second act is two long duets in the cemetery of the Hong Kong Happy Valley. The first between Ysé and her husband, who leaves her on an expedition to Siam; the second between Ysé and Mesa, who, like a greater mystic, has sent the husband to a place of danger in order that the fair Bathsheba may be his own.

But the third act is a surprise. The scene opens

                    To face p. 88

Paul Claudel

in the great first-floor living-room of a European
factory or store in Southern China. It is evening;
all is peace within; Ysé is alone in her white tea-
gown, her yellow hair loosely plaited for the night;
a babe sleeps in its cradle; but without rages the
thunder of cannon with the shrieks of a pillaged
city, sacked by fanatics. The Boxers in revolt
are ravaging the Concession; this sole building, the
strongest, still holds out against them.

To Ysé, anxiously watching, enters her protector;
and, oh, most dramatic surprise !—it is not Mesa;
it is Amalric ! And yet we learn the child is Mesa's.
The man of action has carried off the love and the
son of the dreamer : all the profits of life are for
him. This night the lovers are to die. As club
after convent, store after villa, fall into the hands
of the screaming insurgents, Amalric (ever the
man of action, and even in this tragic hour cheerful,
limited, master of his fate) neatly adjusts the
mechanism of an infernal machine which, before
the Chinese can break down the gates and bolts
of the great factory, will blow the house, its inhabitants, and its assailants high in the air, shattered
to dust in the twinkling of an eye :—

Ysé : Et cependant il est terrible d'être morte.
(*Elle se trouble et lui prend la main.*)
. . . Et, Amalric, est ce que vraiment il n'y a
point de Dieu?

Amalric : Pourquoi faire? S'il y en avait un,
je te l'aurais dit.

But here comes Mesa; he has a pass from the insurgents which permits him to go where he will; he comes to save Ysé. Amalric furious at the sight of his rival, leaps at him with one bound, wrestles with him, flings him off, broken, unconscious, his shoulder out of joint. And he takes from Mesa the talisman which will save their lives, as he has already taken his love and his child. Then, leaving Mesa still in his deep swoon, he carries Ysé down to the harbour, where a ship is waiting, just under the walls.

While Mesa still stirs and murmurs in his swoon, Ysé returns; Amalric thinks her safe in her cabin. But let Amalric live, let Amalric prosper! She will choose rather to die with Mesa in voluntary expiation. Like Gretchen, in Gœthe's *Faust*, Ysé forgoes her chance of life; she will risk the great adventure of Eternity: 'L'esprit vainqueur dans la transfiguration de Midi.' And these last words explain the enigmatic title: Midi, Noon, is earthly passion which must be purified by suffering and sacrifice before it content the soul.

The Sharing of Noon, *Le Partage de Midi*, would make an admirable opera for the music of a Claude Debussy.

To my mind, the most interesting of Claudel's plays, is *L'Otage* (The Hostage), an historical piece in the sense that our poet has captured the atmosphere and character of the period he revives. Though, as for the facts, he invents them at his pleasure. This is the more startling that the time

is 1814, and among the personages are Louis XVIII.
and Pope Pius, whose ghosts must be surprised
to learn some of their adventures.

We are at the end of the First Empire; Napoleon
has the Pope safe in his keeping, a prisoner; so
far so good. But here Claudel parts company with
History. He imagines that a Royalist conspirator,
the Vicomte de Coûfontaine, carries off the Pope
by a deed of derring-do, and conveys him by night
to a half-ruined abbey hidden in the woods of
Picardy—all that is left of his family estate.
Coûfontaine is an émigré, a dangerous exile, with
a price set on his head, and the abbey is inhabited
by a young girl, his cousin, Mademoiselle Sygne
de Coûfontaine, who lives there in great retirement,
striving by endless patience, tireless economy, to
piece again together the tattered fragments of the
family fortunes—not for herself, but for the little
children of that exiled cousin whom, half-unwittingly
she adores.

The opening scene is exquisite : its delicate yet
homely poetry recalls Carpaccio's Saint Ursula
asleep. But Sygne keeps vigil. She is alone by
night in the library of her abbey. The books of
the exiled monks line the walls; on the one side
left bare, a Christ of bronze is nailed to a huge
blackened cross made of the charred beams of
the Château de Coûfontaine, burned under the
Revolution. The tall shuttered windows have no
curtains. There is no carpet on the speckless
floor, where the very nails are burnished. Great

solemn chairs are ranged against the wall. In
one corner, on a wicker hurdle, the harvest of
plums is laid out to dry. In another corner of
the huge bare place the young mistress of the
abbey has established her abode; over her head,
sole ornament, is hung a torn fragment of tapestry,
snatched from the burning, blazoned with the
arms of Coûfontaine. In front of her, a pretty
old-fashioned bureau is covered with ledgers and
files of papers neatly tied. Close by a little table
is spread with bread and wine and the cold meat
for a frugal supper, as though some belated visitor
might be expected.

Coûfontaine arrives in the dead of night; he
brings with him an old nameless priest for Sygne
to house and hide; the girl does not guess it is
the Pope. She greets her cousin with quiet joy,
and with a girlish pride shows him her filed accounts,
her savings, all the store accumulated for the two
exiled children whose miniatures stand on her
writing-table. But both little ones are dead; the
scarlet fever has killed them over in England.
And their mother is dead too, their mother who
had betrayed hearth and home, their mother who
had been the Dauphin's mistress. Coûfontaine is
a desolate man, beset with bitter memories. What
future is there for the race of Coûfontaine? The
scene closes on a betrothal. But (as in Corneille's
Polyeucte) the hearth of plighted love is destined
to be shattered by the stroke of Grace, and the
act of God.

The second act rises on the same background, but it is afternoon. The sun streams in at the uncurtained windows and illuminates the bare room; and the delicate beauty of Sygne, and the figure of ruse and power in front of her. This is her foster-brother, the son of the village sorcerer and of her old nurse; Toussaint Turelure is now a person of importance, one of Napoleon's barons, and Prefect of the Marne. Toussaint Turelure is a vigorous portrait : the vulgarity, the unmannerliness, the ostentation, the parvenu quality of the First Empire are manifest in him; but also its real capacity and power, its grasp of life and men. Toussaint is an Amalric under other circumstances. He loves his delicate and fearless foster-sister even as Napoleon was attracted by the aristocratic Josephine. But so far he has had no hold over her. A woman who asks for nothing and dreads nothing, and cares for nothing, is difficult to terrorise or to seduce. Now Toussaint has surprised her secret : he knows that she has in her keeping the life of Coûfontaine—and that her hostage is the Pope !

So he puts the bargain to her : her hand or their heads ! He gives her two hours to decide on all their fates. And the English readers of Claudel remember William Morris and the 'Haystack in the Floods'—more than once Claudel will remind us of the pre-Raphaelites of yesterday.

The natural woman in Sygne decides for death and freedom. But her parish priest comes to her

and (in a heartrending scene) points out to her
the path of sacrifice. No law, no obligation,
compels a human being to immolate his happiness
to the welfare of the community. Should Sygne,
in the interest of her personal honour, give up the
Pope, no priest dare refuse her absolution : she
is within her rights. But there are rights and
duties superior to our human rights. Man does
not live for man, but for God; and Sygne hears
the voice that, in the midst of his reasoning, surprised the philosopher of Königsburg—the voice
that whispers : 'Du kannst, denn du sollst !'

The third scene rises on the Château de Pantin.
Toussaint Turelure is Prefect of the Seine; he
holds in his hands the destinies of France. A
bevy of Napoleon's officers are drinking the health
of his first-born, whose bells of baptism are ringing
loud and clear—for France has re-entered the
fold of the Church. But the mother is not present
at the festival : the Baronne Toussaint Turelure
is a shattered invalid. Her head, half-palsied,
moves continually from side to side, slowly from
right to left, and again from right to left, in the
weariest gesture of denegation and denial. She is
the wreck of Sygne de Coûfontaine.

While Toussaint drinks and sings with the
Imperial captains, he leaves his sick wife to draw
up a secret treaty with an emissary of the lawful
king of France—for he meditates a timely treason,
à la Talleyrand. Need I say that King Louis's
envoy is the Vicomte de Coûfontaine? Need I

add that their negotiations are varied by the cruel
reproaches of Coûfontaine, by the broken-hearted
disculpations of Sygne. 'Is there anything higher
than Love?' says he; 'is there anything deeper
than one's Race? You have been a traitor to
your heart and your blood.' 'There is God,' says
Sygne,—

'J'ai sauvé le Prêtre éternel.'

But Coûfontaine will not be convinced. At least
he will wreak his vengeance on the usurper. So,
having signed the papers which bring the king to
his own, having carried them off, he takes, through
the open French window, a parting shot at Toussaint
Turelure, which Sygne intercepts, receiving it in
her heart, while Turelure, with a shot of his pistol,
kills the aggressor. Thus the two cousins perish;
their kingdom is not of this world; yet they leave
an heir : a child of the body of Sygne, an heir to
the name and the titles of Coûfontaine by an act
of legal substitution. Like Violaine, like Mesa,
Coûfontaine can leave no child : the hateful Mara,
the brutal Toussaint—brief the children of Action
—can make the fruits of the spirit flourish and
multiply, and they alone.

Why does Sygne save the life of the husband
she never forgives? Is it an act of sacrifice? A
homage to the sacrament? No, for she dies un-
shriven because unforgiving. It is because Death
is better than Life : 'une chose trop bonne pour

que je la lui eusse laissée.' This heartrending
last act of *L'Otage* is especially moving in the
last version, that acted in Paris during the
summer of 1914, in which, mute, dying, relentless, Sygne opposes only silence to the blatant
triumph of her odious master. It is, indeed, the
dialogue of Life and Death.

What will be the ultimate position of Claudel?
It is yet too soon to say. His influence on the
writers of our time is a fact. He is still young;
he is incontestably original; he is no doubt obscure.
But many of the greatest writers were and remain
obscure—Dante, for instance, and Pascal.

In our own times, Carlyle, Browning, Whitman,
Ibsen, Nietzsche, are often mysterious. And
none the less, from the date of their appearance,
they have been read with eagerness, and they
continue to be read (a little less eagerly), and,
indeed, to be revered, as the bearers of a message,
by an undaunted band of followers. Like all
these, Claudel aspires to be a conductor of souls.
And in the things of the spirit a certain obscurity
is no disadvantage, if there be a real message behind
it. We fill out the author's adumbrated meaning,
as we read an intention into a fine musical phrase,
and his sentence gains by all the priceless bulk of
our accumulated interpretations.

There are passages of Shakespeare, there are
Pensées of Pascal, which we contemplate, as it
were, in an atmosphere of moral beauty, a halo, a
luminous aura, through which they shine

transfigured and augmented. They certainly mean more to us than to the most admiring of their contemporaries : their words have been messages to so many passionate and earnest souls ! This phenomenon of accretion is the reward of the obscure : they only, like the saints of Afghanistan, continue to grow in their graves. An Addison, a Voltaire, however great, means what he has always meant. But your obscure genius, in time to come, will be either a gospel or a Gongorism ; there's no third state for him.

FRANCIS JAMMES

FRANCIS JAMMES is a Faun who has turned Franciscan Friar. As we read his early poems, his delicious rustic prose, we seem to see him sitting prick-eared, in some green circle of the Pyrenees, with brown hands holding to his mouth a boxwood flute, from which he draws a brief, sweet music, as pure as the long-drawn note of the musical frog, as shrill as the plaintive cry of some mountain bird who feels above its nest the shadow of the falcon.

And then he met Paul Claudel and was converted.

After all, little was changed, for his innocent paganism had been tinged with natural piety, and in his religion he might say, like the Almighty, in the *Roman de Lièvre*,—

'J'aime la terre d'un profond amour. J'aime la terre des hommes, des bêtes, des plantes et des pierres.'

Only henceforth we see him, in our imagination, like Saint Francis, with a monk's hood drawn over his brow, sandals on his feet, his brown gown cinctured with a knotted cord, a couple of doves hovering over his shoulders, and, at his side, fawning and faithful, a converted wolf. . . .

I met M. Jammes at Madame Daudet's house one winter, and, in fact, his appearance was not wholly unlike this fancy portrait. The gown was a brown woollen suit, but just the Franciscan colour. Above the ruddy, jocund, rustic face, a crown of grizzling curls, behind which Nature had provided the tonsure. Neither dove nor wolf, but, in their stead, all the young Catholic poets of Paris, pressed in serried ranks to meet the Master who, for a few days, had consented to quit his belovèd solitude of Orthez.

We can remember a different Francis Jammes. The poet has said of himself, 'My soul is half the soul of a Faun, and half the soul of a young girl.' But let me quote an admirable strophe from his *Le Poète et sa Femme* :—

'Il est de ceux qui voient les parfums et il sent
    Les couleurs. Et il s'intéresse
Au scarabée cornu, au hérisson piquant,
    Et aux plantes des doctoresses.
Mais le voici, avec sa figure camuse
    Et son sourire de sylvain,
Fatigué par l'amour bien plus que par les muses
    Qui aiment son cœur incertain . . .
Lui-même est un Silène, on le voit au jardin
    Veiller au légume, à la treille. . . .'

This gentle Francis Jammes recalls sometimes the charming La Fontaine, and also Verlaine. A La Fontaine bereft of his philosophy, his deep

knowledge of human nature; a Verlaine from whom
the taint of corruption has been washed and there-
with his terrible sincerity. And if we can imagine
these two great poets mulcted so utterly in their
essential substance, the residue in them, too,
might remind us of a Faun and a young girl—a
mischievous, experienced rustic maid, yet holding
in her arms a bunch of lilies. The first prose study
of our poet—which still remains one of his most
exquisite pages—is the story of a young girl, *Clara
d'Ellébeuse*. What a delightful book ! It is the
sort of little story one can read a dozen times in
a dozen years, and find it as affecting the last time
as the first.

If any attentive student should feel inclined,
having read these pages, to fill a shelf with some
selected volumes of these modern French writers
—with *Colette Baudoche*, for example, from among
the novels of Barrès, and *Antoinette* from Romain
Rolland; with *La Jeune Fille Violaine* from Paul
Claudel; with *La Porte Etroite* from André Gide;
to which he might add *La Jeune Fille Bien Elevéc*
from the works of René Boylesve; *L'Ombre de
l'Amour* by Madame Tinayre; *Marie-Claire* by
Marguerite Audoux; and the young girls of Francis
Jammes, especially *Clara d'Ellébeuse*,—what an
idea, what an admirable, unconventional idea such
a reader would get of the young French girl !
What a gift, at once instructive and delightful, he
could make to some young English girl on, say,
her five-and-twentieth birthday !

Francis Jammes has spent nearly all his life in or near that little town of Orthez (in the department of the Lower Pyrenees), where he was born about 1869. In that part of France, almost as much as in Ireland, Protestants and Catholics divide society pretty equally. Our poet was born and baptized a Catholic, but many of his nearest relations were Huguenots, and, seeing so much of both sides, he does not seem to have taken either very seriously. He showed no particular precocity and, though he began to write poetry, like most people, in his twentieth year, he made his real debut only in 1898, with a volume called *De l'Angelus de l'Aube, à l'Angelus du soir*.

A certain languor mixed with fervour ran in his blood. He had inherited Creole traditions. His grandfather, the doctor, and his grand-uncle had emigrated from Béarn to Guadeloupe, and had settled there, had died there; his father was sent back to France to be educated at seven years of age; his dim memories of the Antilles, his stories of the cousins in Martinique, and the little chair in rare colonial wood that the child had used on the passage, were, a generation later, to set a-dreaming another child, our poet, whose first heroine will belong, like him, to a family dispersed among the Atlantic Islands and the Pyrenees.

I suppose that a doctor would describe Clara d'Ellébeuse as a victim of the *maladie du scrupule*. She is a girl of sixteen; a dear little old-fashioned girl, living in a dear little old-fashioned manor, sheltered among the foothills of the Pyrenees, towards 1848. She has that dread of sin, of impurity, as a sort of quagmire into which one may fall unawares and be lost for ever, which the practice of confession may exaggerate, or palliate, according to the wisdom of the confessor. (Our poet Cowper was no Catholic.) Poor Clara d'Ellébeuse, because one day the young poet she secretly adored had wiped away her nervous tears and laid upon her bowed nape a pitiful, respectful hand, imagines that she has fallen into the sin of unchastity and that she is with child! (And we think of Renan who, in his twelfth year, I think, accused himself in confession of 'the sin of simony.')

The mischief with Clara is that she does not confess; she tells no kind elder of her secret fear; she lets concealment feed, like a worm in the bud, upon her damask cheek. And we know how that ends. Clara does not pine away. One day in March, overcome by horror and remorse for her imaginary crime, she drinks a dose of laudanum and quits this unkind world.

In telling the pathetic history of Clara d'Ellébeuse, Francis Jammes left unhampered that half of his soul which is that of a young girl; but in narrating the fate of *Almaïde d'Etremont, jeune fille passionnée*, that other half (which belongs to a Faun) shows the cloven foot. More tenderly does he commemorate the sad life of *Pomme d'anis, jeune fille infirme*.

But it is not to be supposed that a poet who,

by his own showing, partakes so largely of the
nature of Silenus and his Sylvans, should frequent
exclusively the society of virgins. Some of his
earlier poems betray an ardent sensuality. One
cannot read either these or the *Notes* printed in
the volume called *Le Roman du Lièvre* (or even,
perhaps, that most touching idyll of a play : *La
Brebis Egarée*) without feeling that the poet's
experience has lain also among the lost sheep . . .
among the lost sheep, and perhaps among the
swine; for there was a moment when he was even
as the Prodigal Son !

In 1913, making a general confession of those
past errors (oddly enough) to a reporter of *Le
Temps*, Francis Jammes recalled their bitterness.
Nothing except a love story is so interesting as
the true history of a conversion—I give this one
therefore without apology, though it appeared for
the first time in a newspaper (November 3, 1913).

'Je me suis converti le 7 juillet, 1905, commence
M. Francis Jammes lorsque je lui demande s'il
n'est pas indiscret que je cherche à savoir com-
ment sa pensée évolua de l'indifférence à la ferveur.'

'Vous n'étiez pas catholique?'

'De baptême? Si. Mais pas davantage, avec
des sympathies pour les beaux motifs littéraires
du catholicisme, avec beaucoup de dédain pour
ce que j'appelais, pour ce que je n'appelle plus le
catholicisme des vieilles femmes. J'étais un païen,
un véritable faune. Les fleurs, les bois, les femmes !

J'avais la passion de tout ce qui existait; il n'y avait pas dans toute la nature de gamin plus déchaîné; j'aimais tellement la vie que la seule pensée de la quitter un jour me paraissait un épouvantable blasphème.'

'Et vous ne l'aimez plus?'

'Plus de la même manière.'

'Ce fut un coup de la grâce?'

'Non. Avant la grâce, il y eut les épreuves et il y eut Claudel. . . . Claudel, dont, par l'intermédiaire d'un de ses anciens camarades de classe, Marcel Schwob, je devins l'ami à l'époque faunesque où je battais les buissons . . .

Claudel! Le poète prononce ce nom avec une émotion et une admiration touchantes.

'Claudel! Je n'oublierai jamais, raconte M. Francis Jammes lyrique, ma première entrevue avec lui; il était déjà grand pour quelques-uns d'entre nous. Je vois encore cette petite chambre où l'on nous introduisit, mon camarade et moi. C'était une sorte de cellule nue; trois choses attirèrent mon regard, les seules : un chapelet, l'*Appel au soldat* de Barrès, et un paroissien de vieille femme. Il parut. Le marbre romain allait parler. Il avait de l'antipathie pour la personne qui m'accompagnait : j'entends le son sec et tranchant de ses brèves réponses. Le lendemain je déjeunai avec Schwob et lui. Le marbre, resté glacial la veille, s'anima : ce fut pour moi un émerveillement. Le catholicisme entrait dans ma vie.'

'Le faune avait des inquiétudes?'

'Le faune était tenace. Mais insensiblement je commençais à me demander : où est la vérité? Et de ne pas la connaître, de sentir une limite à l'homme, j'éprouvais une impression pénible, je découvrais un ver dans la pomme. Je m'apercevais qu'il y avait une force dans la vie et que cette force je ne la possédais pas.'

'J'étais dans cet état de désillusion et de doute quand je fus la victime d'une crise morale affreuse. Je tombai dans le désarroi le plus complet. J'avais demandé à un des mes amis de Bordeaux l'hospitalité et je m'abandonnai à ma détresse; c'est alors que par un bienfait de Dieu une lettre de Claudel nous parvint, une lettre admirable de consolation et d'enseignement. Je fus frappé, je réfléchis. Si cette vie que j'aime tant, me disais-je, ne me donne pas son explication, elle n'est qu'une horreur, nous sommes dans un hôpital de fous; j'allai à la cathédrale, longtemps je pleurai : le travail de la grâce s'opérait en moi.

'Je rentrai à Orthez. Ce que la lettre de Claudel avait commencé, la parole de Claudel devait le finir. J'eus bientôt le bonheur de le voir arriver; il me parla du catholicisme en grand philosophe, en savant. · Ensemble nous priâmes. J'étais au fond du fossé, mourant, anéanti. Je me relevai guéri, suavé. Le 7 juillet, 1905, je me confessai, je communiai; Claudel, mon ange gardien, servait la messe. Depuis lors j'ai retrouvé tout ce qui me manquait, j'ai récupéré la joie. Après avoir

traversé d'âpres solitudes, j'ai la joie de la
certitude, l'explication de ma vie. Je suis catholique !'

Dans l'espace, M. Francis Jammes lance cette
profession de foi comme un cri de triomphe.

'Catholique pour de bon, insistai-je, pratiquant?
La foi totale, absolue, obéissante?

'La foi du dernier savetier. Je ne suis pas un
néo-chrétien. Je pratique, comme vous dites,
j'observe tous les préceptes de l'Eglise, ma mère.
. . . Je sais : on rit, vous riez des dévotionnettes.
J'en ai ri jadis moi-même. Je me les suis expliquées.
L'Eglise ne les aurait peut-être pas imposées si
tous les hommes étaient des Pascal et des Claudel.
Mais l'humanité n'est pas composée que de Pascal
et de Claudel. Ces pratiques, ces observances sont
comme des nœuds au mouchoir, elles constituent,
en quelque manière, un rappel à la vertu et à la
piété. L'Eglise les a jugées nécessaires ou utiles.
Je m'incline sans discussion. Cette attitude a
déconcerté certains hommes qui n'ont rien de
catholique mais qui veulent exploiter le catholicisme au profit d'un système politique. Quand
on a la flamme de la foi, comme je l'ai, on trouve
humiliante cette exploitation. Nous, nous sommes
catholiques foncièrement, par-dessus tout.

'Vous parlez comme si vous étiez certain de
posséder la vérité.'

'Je la possède. Je suis dans la vérité puisque
la sécurité où je suis est si bonne! Il n'y a
rien dans le monde à quoi je puisse comparer le

bonheur que ma foi me donne. J'y tiens davantage qu'à la vie elle-même. J'ai été comme un verger où le vent a passé, maintenant je suis un verger doré avec de beaux fruits.

'Et comme j'esquissais un discret sourire de scepticisme, M. Francis Jammes me regarda avec infiniment de générosité.

'Je vous souhaite le bonheur que j'ai.'

'I was converted on the 7th of July, 1905,' began M. Francis Jammes, when I asked him if I were not indiscreet in seeking to trace the progress of his mind from indifference to fervour.

'You were not always a Catholic?'

'I was christened a Catholic, but that was about all: that, and a sort of sympathy for the fine literary themes afforded by the Church, mixed by much disdain for what I no longer call the " churchiness " of old women. I was a Pagan, a veritable Faun! Flowers, forests, women—I was in love with all that lived! In all Nature there was not a merrier young vagabond alive. Life was so delightful in my eyes that the very idea of one day quitting all that, seemed to me a frightful blasphemy.'

'And you are no longer so much in love with Life?'

'Not in the same way.'

'You were changed by a sudden flash of grace?'

'No; there were trials before the Grace of God touched me; and there was Claudel, too, . . .

Claudel with whom I made friends (through one of his old schoolfellows, Marcel Schwob) when I was still a Faun, haunting the thickets.

(Claudel! The poet pronounces the name with a touching admiration and emotion.)

'Claudel! I shall never forget our first interview. He was already a great writer in the eyes of a little clan. I still see the small room into which we were shown, my friend and I. It was a sort of bare cell : three things attracted my attention, a rosary, an old woman's prayer-book, and Barrès's *Appel au Soldat*. And then Claudel came in. It was as if a Roman bust were to move its lips and speak. He disliked the person who accompanied me, and I remember the harsh cut-and-dry tone of his short answers. But the next day I lunched with him and Schwob; and the icy marble softened into flesh and blood. I was lost in wonder, a sort of happy astonishment. Catholicism had entered into my life. . . .'

'The Faun began to feel anxious?'

'The Faun stood firm! But, little by little, I began to ask myself : Where lies the Truth? And the sense of my ignorance, that feeling of a limit to what man can do and be, was the canker in the fruit. I felt there was a force in Life—a force that I did not possess.

'And while in that state of doubt and disillusion, I was overtaken by a cruel moral crisis. I wallowed in the Slough of Despond. One of my friends lived at Bordeaux; I went to stay with him, and it was there that, by God's grace, I received a letter from Claudel. Such an admirable letter, full of consolation and instruction ! I was struck by it. And I pondered it in my heart. "If this dear life," said I, " that I so love, remains a riddle, if there is no answer to our questions, then away with it ! Life is a horror, a madhouse ! " I went to the Cathedral, and for a long while I wept; the miracle of grace began to operate in my soul.

'I returned to my home at Orthez. That which Claudel's letter had begun, speech with Claudel was to effectuate. He came; he spoke to me of religion like a great philosopher, like a man of science, too; and we prayed together. I was in the bottom of the pit, dying, dejected. On the 7th of July, 1905, I went to confession, I received the Communion; Claudel, my guardian angel, served the Mass. Since then I have found all that I missed in life; I have recovered my delight. After the harshest solitudes I have come to a place of certainty : I am a Catholic !'

(And M. Jammes flings this cry forth into space, like a chant of triumph.)

'A real thorough-going Catholic?' said I; 'absolute, obedient faith?'

'The faith of a cobbler ! I am no neo-Christian; I practise all the precepts of the Church I know. You smile (I used to smile) at certain observances. The Church would not have enjoined them if all the faithful stood on the intellectual level of a Pascal or a Claudel. But humanity is not made up of Pascals and Claudels. These minor practices are just knots in our handkerchief, lest we forget ! The Church thinks them necessary; I bow to her decision. I know this attitude seems disconcerting to certain persons, who really are not Catholics at all, but would like to exploit the Church in favour of a political system. But, when the flame of faith is lit in our hearts, we scorn to be the catspaw of a politician. We are just Catholics.'

'You speak as though you were sure of possessing Truth itself !'

'So I am; Truth is my heritage, since I find my security so good ! Nothing in Life is comparable to the happiness which I derive from my religion; it is dearer to me than life itself ! I was as an orchard harassed by the wind; and now I am an orchard golden with ripe fruit.'

So spake Francis Jammes. I smiled the slight smile of the sceptic. The poet glanced at me with an infinite generosity.

'I wish you the same happiness !' he said.

Elie-Joseph Bois, *Le Temps.*
Nov. 3, 1913.

But this conversion has not greatly changed the nature of the poet. His verse is still fresh with the fragrance of wild thyme newly wet with dew. He continues to sing his happy valley, with the mountain towering up behind, right into the blueness of the sky. Only, in his landscape, he gives

more prominence to the village church, gar-
landed with yellow roses : *L'Église habillée de
Feuilles.*

'Par cette grande paix que l'homme cherche en
    soi;
Par les jours finissants aux vieux balcons de bois
Où le cœur noir des géraniums blancs s'attriste;
Par l'obscure douceur des choses villageoises;
Par les pigeons couleur d'arc-en-ciel et d'ardoise;
Par le chien dont la tête humble nous invite
A lui passer la main dessus; par tout cela :
Chapelle, sois bénie à l'ombre de ton bois !'

His verse has still its candour, its ingenuous
freshness, its Franciscan simplicity :—

'Je prendrai mon bâton et sur la grande route
J'irai, et je dirai aux ânes, nos amis :
Je suis Francis Jammes et je vais au Paradis.
Car il n'y a pas d'enfer au pays du Bon Dieu.'

And yet so great a change has necessarily had
its repercussion in the very form of the poet's art :
Francis Jammes is no longer a *ver-librist*. Having
accepted a discipline for his soul, he may well
admit one for his muse. He would no longer
write :—

'J'avais été assez éprouvé pour connaître
Le bonheur de finir ses jours dans la retraite;'

and think he had done his duty by the rhyme.
He would not now content himself with the loose
and lazy assonance of a verse (a beautiful verse)
like the following :—

'Accablé, je m'étais assis, tant les ajoncs
  Étaient impénétrables.
Quand j'eus équilibré mon fusil contre un arbre,
  Je relevai le front.'

His last charming volume of Bucolics, *Les
Géorgiques Chrétiennes*, is written in rhymed Alexan-
drines, which differ only from those of classic
French poetry in a few innocent and agreeable
liberties—a plural and a singular being allowed to
rhyme together, the mute E not counting where
it is not pronounced. It is a pleasant form of
verse. The picture of the harvesting angels whirling
in the sky, which opens the poem, has the rich colour
and the large facility of a fresco by Correggio—
say, the Assumption at Parma. It is beautiful
with a calm beauty :—

'De temps en temps l'un de ces anges touchaient
    terre
  Et buvait à la cruche une gorgée d'eau claire.

'Sa joue était pareille à la rouge moitié
  De la pomme qui est l'honneur de compotier.

'Il reprenait son vol, et d'abord sa faucille.
  Quelque autre alors foulait l'ombre qui fait
    des grilles.

'Ou tous ils descendaient ensemble, ou bien encor
Ensemble reprenaient avec calme l'essor.

'Chacun avait passé le bras à sa corbeille
Dont les tresses formaient comme un essaim
    d'abeilles

'Clarté fondue à la clarté, ces travailleurs
Récoltaient du froment la plus pure des fleurs:

'Ils venaient visiter sur ce coin de la Terre
La beauté que Dieu donne à la vie ordinaire.'

One of my friends, who is Professor of Rhetoric
(Modern Literature) in a High School, tells me
that the enthusiasm of her scholars for Francis
Jammes is a thing touching to behold—for we of
a bygone generation can never quite attain their
diapason. Michelet and Renan leave them cold;
Claudel and Francis Jammes fire their imagination.
If I were a teacher, certainly I should profit by
the experience; by all means let the young learn
from the young!

Les Géorgiques Chrétiennes is full of the most
delightful episodes of country life told in beautiful
(if rather free-and-easy) French. There is no
particular tale in it. It is rather a series of pictures;
the daily life of a family of husbandmen on a farm.
It is a sort of rural *Christian Year*. But what
candid and happy pictures! What a sense of rustic
cheer and frugal abundance! What primitive
poetry in the labourer's account of the creation of

his daily bread; the chestnut, the maize, the vine !
And the betrothal of the little farm servant !
And the vocation of the farmer's daughter who
takes the veil.

There is but one thing in the whole volume
which I find displeasing. It is the short certificate
of orthodoxy which the poet delivers to himself
on the first page and on the last. He is at great
pains to assure us that he is not a reformer, a
philosopher, a modernist, or a free-thinker. We
should never have suspected this gifted and ingenuous singer of being any kind of thinker !
He is a poet, a most indubitable poet, and that
is enough.

RENÉ BOYLESVE

RENÉ BOYLESVE reminds me of some twy-faced
Roman statue, some bust of Janus, turning a
different mask to opposite points of the horizon.
One of these visages (but that regards the Nineteenth Century) has the libertine grace, the refined
scepticism, the voluptuous detachment of an
Anatole France or a Henri de Régnier, with less
philosophy than the one and less poetry than the
other; but these are the qualities which distinguished our Republic yesterday : *Non ragionam
di lor*. The second face looks at the new Renaissance of our time, and is that of an inhabitant
of the province of Touraine, poet and gentleman-
farmer, a man pleasantly occupied with the affairs
of his neighbourhood, in which he finds the diversity,
the unexpected developments, the food for thought,
which animate, in any place, if sufficiently observed,
the innumerable acts of the Human Comedy.

In addition to a mind of the subtlest moral
delicacy and a more than feminine refinement,
M. Boylesve possesses a literary style of transparent
ease and charm; just the style to suit the landscape
he describes, the moderate classic harmonies and
Attic graces of Touraine. He is the historian of
the charming *gros bourgs* that surround Loches or
Azay. He describes their neat, white houses built

of freestone, topped with slate, their raised stone *perrons* (or stoops, as they say in America) and handsome ornamented windows; and we see the trellised vine up the front, and the flowers in the gardens, and the fruit trees everywhere. The villages of Touraine have brought prosperity to to the very brink of poetry!

These little farms where every sunny slope all round is planted with the vine; these old gray manors and priories nestling under some cliff lightly planted with slender oak-woods (so unlike ours!), in which the gray-blue periwinkle and the gray-pink cyclamen grow wild; these prosperous rural properties, with their air of solid comfort, their teeming vats of wine; their kitchen-gardens, full of melons, cucumbers, asparagus, artichokes, cardoons, green peas, egg-plants, tomatoes, salsify, and scarlet-runners; their great barns; their stone stables where the cattle spend so much of their time (for the land is too fertile and too valuable to lay down in pasture); all this dignified, delightful, indolent country of Touraine has found its prophet in René Boylesve. Except Balzac in his *Lys dans la Vallée*, no one has described it half so well—the land and the dwellers on the land . . . 'Molles Turones,' said Cæsar, and Tacitus calls them 'imbelles,' and Tasso thought the peasant here was like his field, which is 'molle, lieta e dillettosa.' And, in fact, these adjectives serve very well to describe the lazy, charming art of René Boylesve.

I find in him the moral features of his race : measure and tact, delicacy of sentiment, love of ease, something at once noble and voluptuous, something humorous and nonchalant, and yet, at the same time, something precise and positive, despite his softness. And often, when I read a novel of M. Boylesve's, the book slips from my hands, and I see the Plain of Touraine under its customary sky of sunny gray—its great wide rivers, its rocky cavernous cliffs, its forests of Loches and Amboise, its rambling lanes sunk deep between two rows of pollard windows, the great straight white high-roads that the aspens fleck with shadow, and all the pleasant sequence of woods and fields, which seem to be reasonably deduced the one from the other, like the different parts of a discourse. Did M. Boylesve know, he would be charmed; for the object of his art is, not to hurry the reader along on a current of breathless events, but to foster in him this habit of reverie, of reminiscence 'chewing the cud of sweet and bitter fancy.'

René Boylesve was born in 1867 at La-Haye Descartes, in Touraine, and his first book, *Les Bains de Baden*, was published in 1896; but this belongs to the Boylesve whom we renounce. In 1899, with *Mademoiselle Cloque*, he opened that series of 'Scènes de la vie de province' (as Balzac would say), which have made his reputation. Mlle Cloque is an old maid of narrow means; just one of those 'churchy' old maids for whom Francis Jammes has expressed a respectful tenderness.

But Francis Jammes was still a 'Faun' when his contemporary, Boylesve, delineated this delightful lady.

Mlle Cloque's affections are divided between two absorbing objects, her pretty young niece and her church. That church is the basilica of Saint Martin, fallen into ruin; and the dearest aim of this devoted worshipper is to restore and repair the great sanctuary of Tours. For to her Tours is still that Jerusalem of the West that our forefathers called it, in memory of the first confessor of the Latin Church, Saint Martin, once the honour and glory of France, neglected now in his own diocese.

Long before Maurice Barrès wrote his apology for the churches of France, the author of *Mademoiselle Cloque* showed how a great monument may be a liberal education, may raise an illiterate mind to heights where it apprehends the mystery which extends beneath, beyond, appearances; he, too, affirmed that the prayer of an old woman in her parish church may rank with the meditation of the man of science and with the inspired presentiment of the poet.

La Becquée followed *Mademoiselle Cloque*. It is impossible to read this long, slow, humorous, enchanting book, without seeing a resemblance (a moral resemblance, for the setting, of course, is widely different since the setting is Touraine), still, a strong moral resemblance to the English novel of Victorian days. Tante Félicie and her nephew,

Riquet Nadaud, remind us, though so unlike, of Aunt Betsy Trotwood and little David Copperfield. It seems to me that those who love the one might, at least, like the other? I shall speak again of Riquet Nadaud in my chapter on the Novel of Childhood.

A great part of the charm of these stories is the atmosphere of Touraine, so marvellously captured. I do not mean only the physical atmosphere : M. Boylesve is above all things a man for whom the inner world is important. Twenty years ago, French literature was positive, objective, and, if I may say so, visual. But now our younger masters are men for whom the invisible world exists; they are chiefly occupied with the interior sphere. Some while ago, René Boylesve described this change of front very happily to a reporter of the *Revue des Français* (September 25, 1912). He said :—

'In my young days, I used to visit Alphonse Daudet whom I greatly admired. He was very encouraging, and we would talk of literature; he used to say to me gently : " I have never described anything that I have not seen." He was very kind, very discreet, and I would go away despairing, for I felt he was offering me a suggestion, a piece of good advice. And for long afterwards I was incapable of writing anything, since at every turn I caught myself on the point of describing things I had never seen, could never see !'

These unseen things—emotions, beliefs, traditions, opinions, all that makes up the moral atmosphere of a society—are the peculiar sphere of M. Boylesve. On this occasion he showed our journalist the plan, or scenario, for a novel which was lying on his writing-table : no project of a plot, no list of personages, but a sequence of maxims and reflections. 'Take care of the moral atmosphere,' he seems to say, 'and the characters will take care of themselves.' So soon as he begins to write, he forgets these notes, which transpose themselves into persons and events; but his preliminary care is to invent the moral world which naturally brings them forth.

The classic grace of his native province, its sober delicacy, its quiet order, do not exclude a latent energy, an amorous ardour, decently dissimulated under the discretion and retinue of a civilised and courtly tradition. The Tourangeau is sensual as well as temperate; he is never perverse; he is seldom excessive ; none the less, if his name be often Descartes or Berthelot, he may by chance be called Ronsard, or Rabelais, or Balzac. How should he live in a world of such good things, such an earthly paradise, and not know—though he discipline them—the pleasures of sense? His purity is not austere and his piety no flaming romantic enthusiasm.

All the delicate sensibility, all this impassioned moderation of his native place, M. Boylesve has put into the human, touching figure of his *Jeune*

Fille Bien Élevée. It is the story of a refined and gentle girl, convent bred, pious, reared in all the old-fashioned dignities and delicacies of a small provincial society in Touraine. Her parents combine for her a sensible match—a *mariage de raison* with a Parisian architect who, visiting Chinon, has espied the white sequestered lily; he marries the dowerless Madeleine for her perfect manners, her charming grace, her moral solidity—*et parcequ'il ne veut pas être.* . . . Poor Madeleine in her wedding veil has overheard the unthinkable word !

M. Serpe has evidently a great opinion of that moral solidity which he so much admires, for, during their married life in Paris, he takes no pains at all to shield it, plunging his young wife into the busy, frivolous circle of contractors, speculators, money-makers, and pleasure-hunters that eddied round the great Exhibition of 1889. This is the subject of *Madeleine, Jeune Femme,* which is the continued history of his heroine—M. Boylesve's novels have the broad full flow and lengthy winding course of his native Loire !

Madeleine passes unscathed among the booths of Vanity Fair. But by a friendly hearth (the one spot which recalls the peaceful surroundings of her early years) she meets a man of letters, a student of subtle moral problems, a lover of Pascal, an inhabitant of her own intellectual world, yet in his private life just as much an average sensual man as any bachelor of the Boulevards. Madeleine succumbs at once almost without resistance to the charm of M. Juillet—she succumbs morally, we mean, and in secret; for in the world of fact she never succumbs at all, and her would-be seducer retires, rebuffed and ashamed, persuaded that she is one of those impregnable fortresses it were a waste of time to besiege, while Madeleine is half enraged by that inalienable aureole, or aspect of virtue, which so efficiently protects her. The flood of sentiment which invades the charmed, the passive soul of Madeleine, its mysterious regression, and the final triumph of her old ideals—Duty, Order, the Interior Altar—are evoked with a magic which touches in the reader's heart a secret spring, and makes him share in Madeleine's temptation, her danger, her reluctant escape.

If Madeleine does not succumb, it was not the beautiful quality of her soul that saved her (our author seems to say) but the regularity and discipline of her early education; and, to point his moral still clearer, he places in front of Madeleine a charming madcap, a dear little modern hoyden, Pipette Voulasne. Pipette has not a bad instinct in her composition, but neither has she a principle; she has never heard of the spiritual combat. Pipette, too, falls in love with the irresistible M. Juillet. Pipette is sweet and twenty, rich, unmarried and M. Juillet is a bachelor; but the lover of Pascal hesitates at the idea of marriage with a romp whose ideas of fun is to dress up as a seal at a fancy ball and swim in the pond.

Pipette is marked out for fate, and here no

sudden angel intervenes; Pipette commits suicide,
—an almost comic suicide, in keeping with her
character; she makes a hearty meal of plum-
pudding and then takes a sea-bath ! M. Boylesve
is a traditionalist, a lover of the ancient faiths and
disciplines of France (a lover, perhaps, rather than
a believer). He delights to show us, in his magic
mirror, the neat, well-ordered world of civilised
society; but sometimes the figures that move
there become transparent, revealing behind them
the great primeval forces, never completely dis-
ciplined, which drop into our neatest systems some
soul irreducibly irregular, a grain of sand throwing
all things out of gear. All his novels are *une
invitation à réfléchir sur la vie.*

There is decidedly something English in the
talent of M. René Boylesve—perhaps his patience,
his slowness, his minuteness, his lambent humour,
as also his repugnance to all that is spasmodic,
jerky, or effective—for sometimes his art reminds
us not only of *David Copperfield,* but also of *The
Mill on the Floss*; and perhaps we must go back
so far to find a novel whose moral effulgence is as
persuasive. A pure and lonely soul, accustomed to
the quiet meditations of the inner life; a young
pilgrim of the ideal, suddenly plunged into the
robust materialism and frivolous worldliness of a
middle-class coterie, abruptly brought up face to
face with passion—with unlawful passion, in which,
none the less, the young soul recognises something
more akin to the altar of her inner worship than

was to be found in the daily round and common
lot; the swift temptation, the sick revulsion.

> 'There came and looked him in the face
>   An Angel beautiful and bright;
> And that he knew it was a Fiend,
>   This miserable Knight!'

Are we not telling the story of Maggie Tulliver?
It is also the history of Madeleine Serpe. It is
her story, with one great, one incalculable difference.
There is an old tale, familiar in many variants
to the students of monastic lore. Tempted, a nun
leaves her convent, errs, returns full of shame, to
find that no one has missed her, that her sin is
unguessed at, since the Virgin has taken her place
and her semblance, performing all her duties in
her place. This interior Virgin, who saves Madeleine
Serpe, who intervenes too late for Maggie Tulliver,
is the habit of goodness, the inheritance and practice
of virtue, which protects some natures half against
their will. For (and there lies the delicacy and
naturalness of M. Boylesve's story) Madeleine's
soul is saved against her will! She feels all the
attraction of the abyss. For one dizzy moment
she leans over, longs—but something pulls her back,
and places her reluctant feet on the dusty highway
they had thought to quit for ever.

.   .   .   .   .

René Boylesve is not one of the greatest names
in contemporary French literature—not a name

to conjure with. No one has ever compared him
to Pascal or Dante, as (to our stupefaction) they
compare Claudel; no one has said of him, as it
has been said of Péguy, that he is greater than
Victor Hugo. And it is as well: this discreet
and moderate artist would find no charm in im-
moderate praise. But we may say without fear
of contradiction that he is one of the most readable
of contemporary novelists.

ANDRÉ GIDE

ANDRÉ GIDE is one of the acutest, one of the most
sensitive critics of the Twentieth Century. His
review, *La Nouvelle Revue Française*, has been no
less indispensible to the development of our younger
writers in France, than the *English Review* to the
Georgian authors across the channel. Instead of Masefield, of Conrad, André Gide has fostered the talent
of a Charles-Louis Philippe, of Marguerite Andoux.

But this critic, so perspicacious, so alert, so
abreast of his times, is, at the same time, a novelist,
apparently of another generation. The Nineteenth
Century in its decline—the dear, delightful, decadent
Nineteenth Century—with its dreams, and its
nihilism, and its irony, and its delicate disenchantment—the Nineteenth Century which already seems
such worlds away !—remains incarnate still in the
novels of André Gide, hardly less than in those of
France, or Régnier, or Pierre Loti. He has the
same sense of beauty, the same regret for some
ante-natal magic never since re-found, the same
perfection of form, or rather a perfection almost
equivalent in its transparent and insidious grace,
in its purity, in its rare elegance : few writers of
the Twentieth Century are elegant ! And, like
Anatole France, Gide, in his latest work, is full of a
bitter contempt, a mordant, an almost impious

derision of human nature. Evil is, in his eyes, the mortar that binds together our earthly tenement; a necessary condition of our being; man is a creature made of dust and mud. But I will not speak of his later books. Of the dozen volumes he has produced, no one is negligible, and at least three, *Paludes*, *L'Immoraliste*, and *La Porte Étroite*, have qualities for which one may suppose survival.

Paludes has a charm of youth and decadence too different from our serious age for me to praise it here; but *L'Immoraliste* and *La Porte Étroite* are as much in earnest as the Twentieth Century can demand, and yet they are not of it !

L'Immoraliste is the story of a young man, newly married, highly gifted, with all his life before him apparently, who suddenly falls sick of a mortal illness. Hitherto he has been a student, spiritually minded, almost austere. But the sudden neighbourhood of death, the dread possibility of annihilation, change his philosophy; he feels that instinctive shudder, that sense of the futility of creeds and conventions which Mademoiselle Lenéru has called *le sens profond de la mort*. And his ideals are reversed.

Henceforth he esteems not the moral, not the refined, but such things as seem especially vital : Life, in such manifestations, bad or good, as appear the most spontaneous, the most energetic. Instinct and Vigour draw him like a magnet, for these make for survival. At Biskra, where he winters for his health, he finds himself admiring the little Arab boy who steals his wife's scissors—the scamp is so adroit, so deft !—and when he returns to his country home in Normandy, it is the drunkards and the poachers in the tavern who strike him as the most alive, and therefore the most estimable. When his wife, worn out with nursing, falls ill in her turn, he neglects her (for illness has become in his eyes disgusting, almost monstrous) and she dies in isolation.

André Gide may be himself, perhaps, something of an Immoralist—or rather an Amoralist—as was the manner of the *Fin-de-siècle*, but he preserves, as the clay preserves the trace of the long crumbled sea-shell, the imprint of a severe and religious education. Like our English Edmund Gosse, he has left behind him a Protestant past, which he looks back upon to-day with some distaste, and yet perhaps with something of an unconscious nostalgia.

His best novel, *La Porte Étroite* (1909), is laid, so to speak, on the grave of that Huguenot youth of his, so utterly vanished, like a handful of flowers.

'Le goût exquis craint le trop en tout.' These words of Fénélon's rise to one's mind in reading this story of a rare soul drawn into the abyss of the inner life, 'as waters are by whirlpools suck'd and drawn,' through a sort of dread of the excess, the commonness, the transitoriness of mortal happiness.

Alissa Bucolin was the child of a West Indian Creole and a Norman banker, Protestant and pious. The beautiful Mme Bucolin never took root in the Huguenot society of Havre; she spent

her days swinging in a hammock or reclining grace-
fully upon a couch, a shut book dropping from her
idle hand; sometimes a violent *crise de nerfs* would
interrupt the languid course of her existence, would
alarm and arouse all the quiet, plain, provincial
household; only sometimes at dusk she would awake
for a moment as it were, show a transient animation, or sit at the piano and begin some slow mazurka
of Chopin; but her lovely hands would stop in the
middle of a chord, her voice leave the phrase
unfinished, and the sleeping beauty sink again into
her incommunicable *ennui*.

Alissa Bucolin drew from her mother her dark
romantic beauty and a neurotic temperament, but
her spiritual strain reflected the cultured Huguenots
of her father's family. Born in the native town of
Mademoiselle de Scudéry (the author of the *Grand
Cyrus*) and of Bernardin de Saint-Pierre (the author
of *Paul et Virginie*), she was akin to the great
précieuse and to the idealist philosopher—and the
likeness makes us wonder if a peculiar morbid
sentimentality, a rare delicacy of emotional fibre,
be usual in the inhabitants of that flourishing
seaport! Alissa had grown up in the companion-
ship of a sister, a brother, and a young boy cousin,
two years her junior—and from their childhood it
had been understood that Alissa and Jerôme were
one day to marry.

But when the girl was sixteen years of age, the
mystery of Evil, and all the scars and scoria of
mortal passion, were suddenly revealed to her by

the conduct of her mother. A novel gaiety and laughter transfigured Mme Bucolin, coinciding with the frequent visits of a certain young lieutenant. And one day Jérôme found Alissa weeping and praying by her bedside while from the floor below her mother's laughter pealed up—unaccustomed as a portent. 'Bucolin, Bucolin,' drolled the young lieutenant, 'Si' j'avais un mouton, sûrement je l'appelerais Bucolin!' and Alissa, weeping, murmured to her dear confidant, 'Jérôme, ne raconte rien à personne . . . mon pauvre papa ne sait rien!'

Thus, in its very bud, the young shoot of love in her heart was infected by shame; and she felt the longing to expiate and offer her life as an oblation. Moreover, Juliette, three years younger than Alissa, had let her fancy light on her young cousin; and the serious Alissa (to whom every preference appeared a vital passion) determined to sacrifice her dream of happiness in her sister's favour. Her strenuous soul was naturally inclined to sacrifice, finding in privation that mysterious exaltation of the will, that constant and progressive self-mastery, which animate with an intense though secret interest the life of the ascetic.

But neither her young sister nor Jérôme would accept her oblation. Juliette married very young a middle-aged wine grower in the south of France, had several children, became her husband's associate, provided an opening for her younger brother —fulfilled, in fact, the French ideal of feminine activity, importance, and devotedness, and was perfectly happy; while Alissa was left (so to speak) with her sacrifice returned unopened, left upon her hands. And Juliette's recovery from her first love, her happiness in a simple marriage of reason, contributed to discredit human passion in the mind of the fastidious Alissa :—

'Ce bonheur que j'ai tant souhaité, jusqu'à offrir de lui sacrifier mon bonheur, je souffre de le voir obtenu sans peine. . . . Juliette est heureuse; elle le dit, elle le paraît; je n'ai pas le droit, pas de raison, d'en douter. . . . D'où me vient, auprès d'elle, ce sentiment d'insatisfaction, de malaise? Peut-être à sentir cette félicité si pratique, si facilement obtenue. . . . Ô Seigneur ! Gardez-moi d'un bonheur que je pourrais trop facilement atteindre !'

To Alissa, as to Mary, the usefulness and occupied content of Martha appear the husks of life : *Unum est necessarium*. Such natures need the liberty, the solitude, the rapt interminable progression, and ideal refuge of the inner life. A sort of disgust of reality seizes them at the very moment when the earthly paradise they dreamed of appears, at last, within their reach. Alissa has only to stretch out her hand in order to take her happiness. After all, is it worth while? The dread of disenchantment, the sense of mortal imperfection, paralyse her. The dawn of love is surely its most delicate, delicious moment; the high day of noon can never improve upon that exquisite suggestion.

'Enough; no more!
'Tis not so sweet now as it was before. . . .'

Those who have once imagined themselves in
direct communication with that which lies behind
appearances cannot resume unaltered the conditions
of human society. Pascal in the full glory of scientific
discovery—and is there any human emotion to
compare with that of the man who suddenly sees
enlarged the very boundaries of Nature?—in the
passion of scientific debate, knew that abrupt
revulsion of the mind, that withdrawal from finite
things, that unique absorption in spiritual perfection
which drove a Charles V. to quit the affairs of
Europe for a monk's cell in Estramadura.

More than once the sense of Divine things has
suggested to a strong nature some cruel doctrine
of voluntary martyrdom, which (according to our
own bias) we may deplore as a partial alienation
of the mind, or admire as evidence of eternal truth.
M. Gide's Alissa is only a woman who renounces a
permitted love; yet, in the same spirit, and with
something of the same high strenuousness, she erases
her dream and writes across the page of life : *Hic
incipit amor Dei*. 'La sainteté n'est pas un choix' (she
tells the unfortunate Jérôme), 'mais une obligation.'

But Alissa was not a saint. She was an artist
in Mysticism, a refined and fastidious spirit 'who
would give all Hugo for a few sonnets by Baudelaire.' Nothing in her life shows that warmth, that
zeal, that desire to rush in and save which marks

the saint, however visionary, however ecstatic, be she Saint Teresa or St Catherine, be he St Francis of Assisi or St Francis of Sales. In place of that simple and passionate impulse of the soul Alissa, in her self-regarding solitude, is all scruple, all a fastidious fear of doing wrong. We think of her, and, opening Fénelon's *Spiritual Letters*, we read :—

'Rien n'est si contraire à la simplicité que le scrupule. Il cache je ne sais quoi de double et de faux; on croit n'être en peine que par délicatesse d'amour pour Dieu; mais dans le fond on est inquiet pour soi, et on est jaloux pour sa propre perfection, par un attachment naturel à soi. . . .'

Over against these strenuous, self-torturing spirits, who arrive with difficulty at perfection, thanks to 'une certaine force et une certaine grandeur de sentiment,' the great Archbishop sets the luminous peace of those quiet souls who glide, as it were, into their true haven, without a conscious effort.

'Tout les surmonte, selon leur sentiment; et elles surmontent tout, par un je ne sais quoi qui est en elles, sans qu'elles le sachent. Elles ne pensent point à bien souffrir; mais insensiblement chaque croix se trouve portée jusqu'au bout dans une paix simple et amère, où elles n'ont voulu que ce que Dieu vouloit. Il n'y a rien d'éclatant, rien de fort, de distinct aux yeux d'autrui, et encore

moins aux yeux de la personne. Si vous lui disiez
qu'elle a bien souffert, elle ne le comprendroit pas.'

We read and reflect that such a friend as this
was just what was lacking to Alissa Bucolin. She
would doubtless have been happier as a Roman
Catholic (only even then she might have chanced
on a Pascal, who would have exasperated her
qualities, instead of on a Fénelon, who would have
tempered and allayed them to a milder perfection).
A spiritual director would have turned her energies
into courses of work and prayer, would have drawn
her mind from the attraction of the abyss, would,
perhaps, have married her (like Juliette) or, more
happily, have fulfilled her vocation in some great
active religious order, where an Alissa may succour
and inspire a multitude of lesser natures. Or, had
the bent to contemplation proved too strong, he
would have let her enter the contemplative life,
but not alone. A soul, scarred by what Sainte-
Beuve has described as *la griffe de l'archange*,
may be seized with a vertigo, on attaining the
summits of the inner world, if on these giddy
heights no staying, guiding, protecting hand be
near. *Vae soli!*

But in that case Alissa would not tragically have
died, leaving behind a long train of sterile regret
and hopeless memories, and M. Gide would not
have composed the frail and spiritual story, which,
in its purity and charm, reminds us sometimes of
Dominique.

CHARLES PÉGUY

WHEN war broke out between Austro-Germany and the Allies, Charles Péguy went to the front as a lieutenant in the reserves of the line and was struck by a ball, or a fragment of shell, on the forehead as he was leading his men into action at the Battle of the Marne. This heroic death fitly crowns a career devoted to the love of country and the gospel of fraternal self-sacrifice.

In its light, I re-read the trivial pages, the feeble half-affectionate pleasantries with which I had saluted the poet and teacher who, no doubt, occasionally abused the privilege which genius sometimes claims to alloy the sublime with the ridiculous—or the merely ultra-lyrical and wearisome. Is it possible that I did not appreciate, in his lifetime, the prophet, the hero, the poet, whom France reveres to-day? I examine my conscience. It is clear that I was not drawn to Péguy in his habit, as he lived. . . . I see him still. An odd little man with the look of a small farmer from the Loire —a farmer, a village schoolmaster, a country doctor, a curé even—there was something of all that in the refined and yet rather common little man with the bent shoulders, the charming hands, the square jowl, and the deep-set blue eyes whose glance was

at once so keen and so gentle, often so quizzical,
sometimes so mystically tender, and sometimes so
irritable and angry.

'Un petit homme barbu (said Barrès) un paysan,
sobre, poli, circonspect, défiant et doué du sens
de l'amitié, bien campé sur la terre, et toujours
prêt à partir en plein ciel. C'était un petit homme
terne et lent, de qui se dégageait un merveilleux
rayonnement.'

He seemed to me like some preaching friar of
the Middle Ages, vowed to Dame Poverty; and,
for himself, content with a crust in his wallet,—
a wretched living picked up as he went along the
roads, yet, where his Order was concerned, insatiable,
a relentless beggar for the Love of God. Pitiless
to any human hobby or pursuit of yours which
did not square with that sublimer hobby and
pursuit of his; himself disinterested, and yet in
his ardent piety as dauntless an intriguer as any
Jesuit of Eugène Sue's; cordial and frank by fits
and starts, with that engaging air of rustic simplicity and popular plain-dealing, yet, on the
morrow, infinitely wily, full of craft, subtlety, and
innocent guile. I thought him (notwithstanding
the mysterious, irradiating kindness which beamed
from that wonderful glance of his) on the whole
a crotchety creature, 'difficile à vivre,' with a
temper full of sudden twists and turns and unsuspected asperities.

Admirable he was, nevertheless. Patient as a peasant and courageous as an apostle, wise and witty, bitter and gay, Péguy was full of sense and of charity—was almost that rarest of geniuses, a saint—and failed there (remaining merely a poet and a hero) chiefly, perhaps, because of that insatiable vanity of his. He hungered and thirsted not only after righteousness, but after praise. And in his lifetime he never had his due share of it. That meed so scantily meted I might in some small degree have swelled, and now regret my suspended judgment; but Péguy roughed me up in every fibre, and I disapproved of him almost as much as I admired him. There was something of Rousseau in the fiery little autodidact with his penetrating delicacy of sentiment, and that sore vanity of his as touchy as a gouty foot which always fears the man across the way may stumble on it. When that aching place was hurt, the poet, so exquisite in his sense of friendship, so abundant in his recognition of encouragement, would surprise those most who knew him best by certain restive or morbid quarrels—the blemishes of a too sensitive temperament.

Despite this temperament, which was not great, there was something really great and grand in Péguy. There was in him the most generous passion of rescue—the desire at all risks to rush in and save. The grandeur and misery of Man and his need of salvation was the idea which dominated all his life. Péguy was a mystic; Time was nothing to him, and he was sincere in saying that an act of rescue such as that which cost him his life was worth a career of thirty years. Yes, Péguy was a mystic, and one of the real, the greater race, no romantic idealist, not at all vague or dreamy, but positive and practical and intensely alive to every detail, because every fact in nature (and indeed all the best things in industry and in art) appeared to him, in Meister Eckhart's phrase, 'the words of God,' and therefore infinitely precious and important. One day that his friend and mine, Daniel Halévy, that subtle and yet substantial critic, found him reading Dante's *Paradiso*, in view of a certain Mystery he meant to write : Le Propre de l'Espérance (and the part, the lot, of Hope is Paradise), M. Halévy asked the audacious poet if those whirling worlds of Dante's and all those whorls of singing aureoled angels did not inspire him with at least a certain vertigo? 'Not at all,' replied Péguy. 'My Paradise will be quite different.'

'"Il y aura dans mon Paradis des choses réelles. . . . Toutes les cathédrales." . . . Et il faisait avec les deux mains le geste d'y poser quelque chose. "Je les y mettrai."'

And in fact (continues M. Halévy in the letter from which I am quoting) Péguy would have admitted to his Paradise, not only the great Cathedrals, but anything perfect in its own peculiar sphere. For instance, he adduces :—

'this ink with which I am writing to you, which indeed was Péguy's ink, made of the oak, coal-black, indelible; and his pens—they too would have gone into his Paradise, certainly, all his pens! You have understood I am sure; Péguy extends the future life, not only to souls and sentiments, but to all that has achieved existence; a resurrection not only of the flesh but of the things made, cherished, and perfected by man on earth.'

It was more or less Swedenborg's Paradise. In Péguy's eyes the soul vivified and transfigured and made alive all that it touched. Hence his utter incomprehension of all attempts to examine matter that the soul had *not* transfigured, his withering contempt for science and scientists, the scorn he would pour on those miserable insects, the 'puissants millepieds' of the University, in their laboratories and archives :—

'Et ce ne sera pas ces distingués cloportes
Qui viendront nous chercher dans notre enterre-
    ment. . . .
Et ce ne sera pas par leur usage externe
Que nous nous lèverons de notre pourriture;
Mais la Foi qui nous sauve et seule nous discerne
Saura nous retrouver dans la fange et l'ordure.'

(Eve.)

What discussions I have had with Daniel Halévy concerning the final value of this poem of *Eve*, whose mighty jog-trot extends interminably over a length which exceeds the *Odyssey* and the *Iliad* together ! My friend, to whose opinion I attach the greatest weight, insists on ranking Péguy with Victor Hugo for poetry and with Rabelais for prose ! And no doubt he emphasises his expressions in order to spur my tranquil spirit to the fray. Indeed the incitement never yet failed of its effect; I rush to the encounter; sometimes, at the point of the bayonet, M. Halévy recedes from his position as regards Victor Hugo; but he maintains unshaken that comparison with the creator of Pantagruel.

Well, all that is vain; Péguy now will never fill his measure. His monument is a broken column, like those we see in cemeteries. In these brief passages of recollection, I may not even stay to point out the extraordinary design and intention of that monument; nor to quote that prose, surely unlike any other prose, which creeps up, wave after wave, with infinite repetitions and over-lappings, until, like the tide on the strand, it has submerged and sucked in all the subject it meant to cover. How, in two words, could I give an idea of that style?

Péguy is a great prose writer, a wonderful wielder of image and trope, a master juggler with all the intricacies of French syntax. And the nation which produced Agrippa d'Aubigné, Pascal, Voltaire, has always loved the prose of a brisk polemic. The prose works of Péguy are due to polemics. And he lays into his enemy with a dexterity, a surety, a variety of attack unrivalled—here a shower of swift and sudden blows, there a slow and paralysing envelopment of the adversary. Péguy is an incomparable wrestler.

For the rest, shall we say that Péguy was the Walt Whitman of France? Shall we translate him into English under the name of Carlyle—or even W. E. Henley? There was something of all of them in the irascible, quizzical, and lovable idealist whose life was one long struggle against conventional standards and a conventional style; against middle-class prosperity, modern commodities (generally 'tout le confort moderne'); against the preferences of a well-to-do democracy; against also, and no less, Parliamentary ideals; documentary historical methods and culture; and, compendiously and inclusively, all that is political as opposed to mystical, all that is temporal as opposed to spiritual, all that is matter as opposed to soul, all that is personal as opposed to general, and, one may add by extension, all that is rich as opposed to all that is honourably, contentedly, and modestly poor.

With these dispositions it is natural that Péguy should have begun life as a Socialist. Born of humble stock in 1874 (on those prosperous banks of Loire where the humblest have all things pleasant and comely about them, and are themselves men of a slow, wise wit and kindly culture) Péguy rose from class to class, from board school to training college, until at twenty he found himself at the University of Paris, one of the future glories of the Ecole Normale. In the old house of the Rue d'Ulm he wrote his first poem, *Jeanne d'Arc* (for

already this son of Orleans was possessed by the
memory of the Maid), of which the singular dedication reflects not only his young ideas of fraternal
democracy, but that extraordinary tide-like style,
creeping on inch by inch, wave by wave, until it
submerge the whole ground of the matter, which
Paris, in later days, was so often to admire, to
praise, or to deride :—

'A toutes celles et à tous ceux qui auront vécu,
A tout celles et à tous ceux qui seront morts
    pour tâcher de porter remède au mal
    universel;
En particulier,

'A toutes celles et à tous ceux qui auront vécu
    leur vie humaine,
A toutes celles et à tous ceux qui seront morts
    de leur mort humaine,
    pour tâcher de porter remède au mal universel
    humain.

'Parmi eux,
A toutes celles et à tous ceux qui auront vécu
    leur vie humaine,
A toutes celles et à tous ceux qui seront mort de
    leur mort humaine
    pour l'établissement de la République Social-
    iste universelle,
    ce poème est dédié.
Prenne à présent sa part de la dédicace qui
    voudra !'

'Tâcher de porter remède au mal universel humain': To attempt to ease the universal disease of humanity! All Péguy is there! As time went on, he ceased to believe in the establishment of the universal Socialist Republic; and, indeed, although ineradicably attached to the Republican ideal, he became increasingly anti-radical, anti-democratic, almost tending towards the military, and aristocratic theory of a State strongly constituted in definite classes, each respectable, respected, and informed with the same sense of national honour and personal self-sacrifice. But Péguy went back on no word of that early dedication. He simply made over, so to speak, his stock in the universal Socialist Republic to the credit of the Catholic Church. For before Claudel, before Francis Jammes, after Brunetière (or we should rather say along with him) Péguy suffered a conversion to the faith of his fathers.

Yet such was his respect for the individual conscience, that he continued, in the eyes of the Church, to live in sin. His wife, the daughter of a Socialist, was a Free-thinker; she had never been baptized; she had married Péguy before the Mayor of her Commune and not before the priest of her parish; she had not followed him in his conversion and still maintained her rights. Péguy, that arch-persuader, could not shake her. And, since the indissolubility of the marriage-tie was the very cornerstone of Péguy's social doctrine, he continued to live with this free-souled woman, who shared his life but not his faith, in an unblessed union, that the Church condemned; his children were not baptized. Rome bade him bring them into her fold. Péguy, in his pride of *pater-familias*, upheld his claim to consider the convictions of their mother. Deprived of the sacraments, he ceased to go to Church, while still continuing to believe and pray. . . . Anti-clerical and ardently Catholic; tenderly preoccupied with his children's welfare and yet accepting for them that which his new-found creed must have made him conceive as the most dreadful risk of all—such was the stubborn and irascible convert whom the Church honours in his death, but whom in his lifetime she covered with reprimands and ardent reproaches.

Such was Péguy in his life—an enigmatic being; nor was he less difficult to appreciate in his art, which attempts to enlarge our sensibility and quicken our moral vision much in the same way as instantaneous photography has increased and instructed our sense of sight. I am the first to concede that this art of his (which proceeds, perhaps, rather from Dostoieffsky than from any great French tradition) appears, in its disconcerting diversity, as one of the most interesting phenomena of a new age. It is full of audacity, interest, genius, adventure. But is it an art? Let us open any page of Péguy and take at random a charming page, where the book opens, p. 63 of the *Porche de la Deuxième Vertu* :—

'Et pourtant on est si fier d'avoir des enfants !
(Mais les hommes ne sont pas jaloux) :
Et de les voir manger, et de les voir grandir.
Et le soir de les voir dormir comme des
     anges.
Et de les embrasser le matin et le soir et à
     midi.
Juste au milieu des cheveux.
Quand ils baissent innocemment la tête comme
     un poulain qui baisse le tête.
Aussi souples comme un poulain, se jouant
     comme un poulain.
Aussi souples du cou et de la nuque. Et de
     tout le corps, et du dos.
Comme une tige bien souple et bien montante
     d'une plante vigoureuse.
D'une jeune plante.
Comme la tige même de la montante espér-
     ance !
Ils courbent le dos en riant comme un jeune,
     comme un beau poulain, et le cou, et la
     nuque, et toute la tête.
Pour présenter au père, au baiser du père, juste
     le milieu de la tête.
Le milieu de la tête, la naissance, l'origine, le
     point d'origine des cheveux.
Ce point, juste au milieu de la tête, ce centre,
     d'où tous les cheveux partent en tournant,
     en rond, en spirale.
Ça les amuse ainsi.
Ils s'amusent tout le temps.'

The volume, the sensitiveness, the stammering reiteration, the precision, the tenderness, the subtlety of Péguy are all in this passage. One would say an artist of genius, afflicted with general paralysis, attempting to describe a miraculous vision. And he is telling us that a father kisses his small boy on the crown of his cropped little pate. And this passage of Péguy's is no more extraordinary than any other passage of Péguy's on any other possible subject. Imagine Walt Whitman turned a Christian mystic and endowed with ten thousand times his original flux of words.

And now, having relieved my soul, having put the accent on this intolerable defect of our poet's —and it is almost, to my thinking, a redhibitory vice—let me turn to his bright side and discover what it is that attracts to him so many and such distinguished admirers.

It is, first of all, a touch on the canvas, a liquid and a living palette, an animation and abundance of composition which, in his too rare happy moments, suggest some large and brilliant sketch of the school of Rubens. Take the opening quatrains of the poem to which I have referred; let us open *Eve* :—

'O mère ensevelie hors du premier jardin
Vous n'avez plus connu ce climat de la grâce,
Et la vasque et la source et la haute terrasse,
Et le premier soleil sur le premier matin.

Et les bondissements de la biche et du daim
Nouant et dénouant leur course fraternelle,
Et courant et sautant et s'arrêtant soudain
Pour mieux commémorer leur vigueur éternelle.

There is, in Péguy at his best, something not so
much antique as unchanged since ancient times,
like the pronunciation of certain peasants; and
this something makes us understand how there
once was in France a people of artists, the unknown,
unnamed, immortal builders of the great Gothic
cathedrals; we almost believe there might still be
such in reading his verse.

There is also in Péguy at his best a peculiar
humanity which makes me often remember those
lines of Mrs Browning concerning her favourite
Greek poet :—

'Our Euripides the Human
With his droppings of warm tears,'

and an imagination so naturally and naïvely
religious that it would enchant me but for its
familiarity. No Baptist minister over his tea and
muffins, is on more intimate terms with the Eternal.

The interminable poem of *Eve* (as long—but
not as beautiful! as the *Iliad* and the *Odyssey*
united) fulminates against the Intellectuals of
France in an outburst of rhetoric which too often
degenerates into mere violence. Péguy is more
really poetic in his prose. The description of rural

life on the banks of the Loire, in *Victor-Marie,
Comte Hugo*; the death of Bernard Lazare in *Notre
Jeunesse*; above all, the long but the inspired
elevations and prayers of Jeannette—especially
the conversation with her little fourteen-year-old
friend Hanorette (which we keep in our remembrance along with the dialogue of Antigone and
Ismene, and with the scene in the Gospel of Martha
and Mary, as a perfect characterisation of the two
great types of Charity and Piety)—are to our
thinking far more interpretative of Péguy's true
genius than the mighty jog-trot of his later muse.
Still there is a power and an eloquence in that.
So far as the meaning goes, all his voluminous out-
pourings have the same. There is but one thing
needful, and that is to be a hero or a saint. Prefer-
ably, perhaps, a hero!

'Ainsi Dieu ne sait pas, ainsi le divin maître
    Ne sait quel retenir et placer hors du lieu,
Et pour lequel tenir, et s'il faut vraiment mettre
    L'amour de la patrie après l'amour de Dieu.'

The saints that Péguy sang were patriot saints:
Geneviève, who preserved the city of Paris from
the Huns of Attila; Jeanne, who hunted the English
out of France. Of all glories, of all honours, that
dearest to this poet was military glory and national
honour—

'Il n'y a rien à faire à cela, et il n'y a rien à
dire. Le soldat mesure la quantité de terre où

on parle une langue, où règnent des mœurs, un
esprit, une âme, un culte, une race. Le soldat
mesure la quantité de terre où une âme peut respirer.
Le soldat mesure la quantité de terre où un peuple
ne meurt pas.

This was Péguy's firm conviction : no duty so
important as the military duty ! When the war
broke out, man of forty as he was and father of
a struggling family—man, too, much engrossed
and overworked by his triple occupation as poet,
prose-writer, and publisher—he changed from the
Territorials into a regiment sent on active service
to the front. 'No man hath greater love than
this. . . .'

Thanks to the recital of one of his soldiers, Victor
Bondon, we can witness the fall—or rather I would
say the assumption—of the poet and brother of
Joan of Arc. For he too fell in driving the invader
out of France ! There is an extraordinary breath
of heroism in this page of an unknown private
soldier relating the end of a great man. I cannot
do better than translate it here, with some abridg-
ments and suppressions :—

'On the 5th September in the morning, the
55th division of the army of Paris was ranged on
the left of the forces which had received the general
order, " Die where you stand, rather than retreat."
In front of us, on the wooded hills that reach
from Dammartin to Meaux, von Klück and his

Boches, who had followed us step by step from Roye during our terrible retreat, lay in wait for us, hidden in their trenches, like beasts of prey.

'The heat was tropical; the battalion halted a moment at the pretty village of Nantouillet. I see again, with the mind's eye, our dear Lieutenant Péguy, seated on a stone, white with dust (as indeed we all were), covered with sweat, his beard rough and shaggy, his eyes shining behind his pince-nez. Such he was, as we had seen him in Lorraine during the retreat, impervious to fatigue, brave under a storm of shells, going from one to another of his men with a cheering word for each throughout the whole length of our company (the 19th), sharing our rations (and we eat as a rule one day in three), never complaining despite his forty years, as young as the youngest, knowing just the right way to take the Parisians that we were, heartening the discouraged with a word, satirical enough some-times, but more often a friendly quizzical quip, always brave, always an example; ah, yes! I see again our dear lieutenant, bidding us fight in hope, raising our flagging spirits in an hour when many were near despairing, with the assurance of his own absolute confidence in our final victory.'

'At last the sun began to slope towards evening; it was five o'clock. After four hours' incessant fire, our 75's had silenced the Prussian batteries on the ridge, and the infantry were ordered to attack their entrenchments. The black troops from Morocco, in what had seemed an invincible rush, had tried once, and failed. Now Péguy's company starts in skirmishing order; the German batteries are quiet, but when our men reach the ridge they are greeted by a storm of bullets. The ground is covered with tangled, down-trodden oats that catch the feet; and in front, just on a level with their heads, that burst of fire. Péguy's voice, ringing and glad, commands the assault : " Feu ! En avant ! . . .

'Ah ! cette fois c'est fini de rire. Escaladant le talus et rasant le sol, courbés en deux, pour offrir moins de prise aux balles, nous courons à l'assaut. . . . Le capitaine Guérin, M. de la Cornillière, sont tués raides, " Couchez-vous (hurle Péguy) et feu à volonté ! " mais lui-même reste debout, la lorgnette à la main, dirigeant notre tir, héroïque dans l'enfer.

'Nous tirons comme des enragés, noirs de poudre, le fusil nous brûlant les doigts. . . . Péguy est toujours debout, malgré nos cris de " Couchez-vous," glorieux fou dans sa bravoure. Le plupart d'entre nous n'ont plus de sac, perdu lors de la retraite, et le sac, en ce moment, est un précieux abri. Et la voix du lieutenant crie toujours : " Tirez ! Tirez ! Nom de Dieu ! " D'aucuns se plaignent : " Nous n'avons plus de sac, mon lieutenant, nous allons tous y passer ! " " Ça ne fait rien ! (crie Péguy dans la tempête qui siffle). Moi non plus ! Je n'en ai pas, vous voyez. Tirez

toujours!" Et il se dresse comme un défi à la
mitraille, semblant appeler cette mort qu'il glorifiait
dans ses vers. Au même instant, une balle meur-
trière fracasse la tête de ce héros, brise ce front
généreux et noble. Il est tombé, sans un cri,
ayant eu l'ultime vision de la victoire proche; et
quand, cent mètres plus loin, bondissant comme un
forcené, je jette derrière moi un rapide coup d'œil
alarmé, j'aperçois là-bas, comme une tache noire
au milieu de tant d'autres, le corps de ce brave,
de notre cher lieutenant.'

And here for a threnody let me quote that noble
psalm, now familiar to the soldiers of France,
which, until Péguy's death, lay hidden in that vast
storehouse of lumber and treasure, the poem of
Eve. Be sure it will remain for ever among the
ultimate residue—the pure regulus—of all that nas
been written on the war. And these stanzas were
written before the battle was declared, since Péguy
(and therein lies his true grandeur) was a prophet
rather than a poet.

'Heureux ceux qui sont morts pour la terre
     charnelle,
Mais pourvu que ce fût dans une juste
     guerre;
Heureux ceux qui sont morts pour quatre coins
     de terre,
Heureux ceux qui sont morts d'une mort
     solennelle.

'Heureux ceux qui sont morts dans les grandes
    batailles,
Couchés dessus le sol à la face de Dieu;
Heureux ceux qui sont morts sur un dernier
    haut lieu
Parmi tout l'appareil des grandes funérailles.

'Heureux ceux qui sont morts pour des cités
    charnelles,
Car elles sont le corps de la cité de Dieu;
Heureux ceux qui sont morts pour leur âtre et
    leur feu
Et les pauvres honneurs des maisons paternelles.

'Heureux ceux qui sont morts, car ils sont
    retournés
Dans la première argile et la première terre;
Heureux ceux qui sont morts dans une juste
    guerre;
Heureux les épis mûrs et les blés moissonnés !'

'Qui Dieu mette avec eux dans le juste plateau
Ce qu'ils ont tant aimé : quelques grammes de
    terre;
Un peu de cette vigne, un peu de ce coteau,
Un peu de ce ravin sauvage et solitaire.

'Mère, voici vos fils qui se sont tant battus !
Qu'ils ne soient pas pesés comme Dieu pèse un
    ange :
Que Dieu mette avec eux un peu de cette fange
Qu'ils étaient en principe et sont redevenus. . .

And, as we say a collect after singing an anthem, let us conclude, in memory of all those heroic comrades that fell with Péguy in the battle, with a noble passage from his *Mystery of the Holy Innocents* :—

'Une génération d'hommes (dit Dieu).

'Une promotion, c'est comme une belle longue vague qui s'avance d'un bout à l'autre sur un même front et qui d'un seul coup d'un bout à l'autre.

'Toute ensemble déferle sur le rivage de la mer.

'Ainsi une génération, une promotion, est une vague d'hommes.

'Tout ensemble elle s'avance sur un même front.

'Et toute ensemble elle s'écroule comme une muraille d'eau quand elle touche au rivage éternel.

Thus Péguy died with the generation that he led to victory.[1]

[1] I refer those of my readers, who wish to learn more of Péguy, to my friend Daniel Halévy's volume : *Charles Péguy et les Cahiers de la Quinzaine*, Payot et Cie, Paris, 1919.

ERNEST PSICHARI

I THINK that Péguy never learned the death of his young friend, Ernest Psichari; for the retreat of Charleroi was, after all, such a little while before the battle of the Marne, and news in those difficult days travelled so slowly. . . . One of Péguy's last preoccupations was the hope of meeting Ernest on the road to battle, and in fact they must have been in Lorraine together, but no chance encounter by road or rail set the two friends face to face. They both started for the front in the same mood of heroic exaltation :—

'Si je tombe (said Péguy), ne me pleurez pas. Ce que je vais faire vaut trente ans de travail.'

But the first to fall was Ernest Psichari. I knew him root and branch—knew his parents and grandparents before him, and the earliest image that I preserve of him (since the first of all are forgotten) is of a little lad between eight and nine years of age, unaware of my presence in his grandmother's drawing-room, as he talks to his little brother in the twilight : 'When I am grown up (says Ernest) I shall be a great man ! Et j'aurai ma statue sur tous les marchés de France !' And the little one of seven ripples with laughter at Ernest's having so satisfactorily 'gone one better' : 'Il y a du chemin à faire, mon frère ! (says he).

Il y a bien de chemin à faire !' Whereat I too laughed and broke the spell, the two little boys informing me that, while waiting for their violin-lesson, 'on s'amusait à raconter des blagues.'

Even in Ernest's fun there was a desire of greatness; that, and an intense sensibility, a rare faculty of moral imagination, were what I chiefly noticed in the child, of whom I saw less and less as his studies absorbed him more and more : youths between twelve and twenty have little time for their mother's friends. A quiet young man, with charming, living eyes, and in his whole aspect something ardent, firm, and grave : that is all that Ernest Psichari was to me.

And then came a bolt from the blue. It was on the morrow of the Dreyfus case when France was divided into two camps, and each faction feverishly counted its men and the great families which centralised these men on either side. As Daniel Halévy wrote, in a passage already cele-brated : 'Paris a ses familles comme Florence eut les siennes, et ses maisons, non couronnées de tours, n'en abritent pas moins des factions guerrières.' Ernest was born into one of these houses—one of the most important to the Liberals—for those grandparents of his (both dead before that shock of schism shook France to her foundations), those grandparents of whom I have written, were Ernest Renan and his wife. And his father was Jean Psichari, a Greek philologist of most 'advanced' opinions. It came, therefore, almost as a defection, an apostasy, when the rumour spread in the ruffled circles of the Dreyfusards that Ernest Psichari had gone into the Army—that Renan's grandson, at nineteen, had enlisted as a volunteer in the Colonial Artillery.

Although myself a Dreyfusard with the best of them, I could not feel hurt by this change of front, which seemed to me just the counterpart of Renan's own conversion. Given a young man with a passion for justice, the more you treat him as a partisan, the more his mind, by some dim process of unconscious cerebration, will conjure up the arguments for the other side. Besides Renan, although he gave his casting vote to the Liberals, exhaled often an exquisite regret in his vision of the other side. He finally voted for Caliban; but few writers have set forth more nobly the arguments for the aristocratic ideal. Renan's mind was singularly full. Imagine a pair of scales, either balance heaped high,—even the lighter of them was filled with more reasons to believe, to rule, and to conquer than many a fanatic could furnish forth; it is true the reasons for doubting turned the scale. The man who sacrificed everything to Truth and Liberty was just the man to understand the young apostle of Force and Faith; he too had felt the spell of Force and Faith ! Ernest Psichari—grave, straightforward, active, patient—represented the France of to-day in its modern cult of sacrifice and duty, even as the grandsire stood for his own generation. The symbols are different, but the character is much the same—a like curiosity, an equal contempt for worldly goods and mundane honours, a conviction that life is worth living only when employed in some vast impersonal service. The wise Merlin of the Nineteenth Century would have smiled: 'ah! cher enfant, combien vous avez raison!'

'Le fils a pris le parti de ses pères contre son père'; so Ernest himself defined the situation in his *Appel des Armes*. Just as his Breton ancestors, curious of the vast world on the other side the seas, most incurious of worldly advancement, would sail the world over in the Service of the State, before the mast, seamen content with the salt air and their duty, so this grandson of theirs spent five years with his cannon in the Congo, a non-commissioned officer. When at twenty-four years of age he returned to Paris, he could scarcely understand why his friends pressed him to enter a school for officers. 'One can serve the country as well in the ranks; one is perhaps more useful!' But he yielded to his mother—to her, indeed, he always yielded.

How I regret that during those eighteen months which the young soldier spent at Versailles, in order to obtain his brevet of second-lieutenant, I remained unaware of his presence in France! Péguy has left an eloquent description of his friend and young alumnus, telling how he lived like a king in the palace of the Ecole Militaire, but a step from the dome of the Invalides whither in the summer mornings, in the freshness of the dawn, he used to escort his slender little three-inch cannon

—'ses 75, ces petits jeunes gens de canons modernes, ces gringalets de canons modernes, au corps d'insecte, aux roues comme des pattes d'araignées' —filing them off under the shadow of the monstrous historic artillery of the great Pensioners' Hospital, the cannon of Fontenoy and Malplaquet, bronze mastodons and leviathans of an earlier age. I can imagine Ernest, 'l'homme au regard pur' (as Péguy calls him); I can see him, a young Hippolytus of the School of War, in my mind's eye —but I did not see him in the world of facts. Before I learned of his presence in my neighbourhood he had left—he and his battery—for the deserts of Mauritania, and there, in the desolate tropical country that lies between the burning plains of Senegal and the sands of the Sahara, he spent three happy years. He sent home a little book—*Terres de soleil et de sommeil*—which marked the awakening of his literary gift; but the real event of those three years, for Ernest, was his ardent conversion to the Catholic Church. Ernest was a mystic; the only life possible to his insatiable heart was the spiritual life; and in the Sacraments he sought that assurance of a world beyond our own, in constant communication with our own, which other minds may find by other means. His fervour, his faith, was henceforth a remedy for all his sins and all his sorrows; and, young as he was, he had had his sorrows—doubtless, also, his sins.

It was, I think, in the end of 1912 that Ernest left that immense and mortal splendour of the

Sahara and came back to France, bringing with him a short military novel, *L'Appel des Armes*, which (coming after Péguy's elaborate pæan) received, on its publication in 1913, an honourable, a more than honourable, welcome. . . . I was one of the welcomers. Few things are pleasanter to the hoary critic than the *éclosion* of a fresh young talent, and naturally all the more when that talent flowers on a dear familiar stem. On this occasion I renewed my long-interrupted friendship with the young author, and we promised ourselves a more frequent communication of our ideas. Fate however, decided otherwise. Ernest and his battery were sent to the cliffs of Cherbourg. And, a year later the great war began. . . .

Thus it happens that Ernest Psichari's fame must rest on three small volumes, of which the finest by far appeared after his death—that *Voyage du Centurion*, which is the unforgettable record of a mystic's conversion in the blazing African desert. There is less genius and less force in this earlier, tiny volume called *l'Appel des Armes*, so full of inexperience, of an ardent evident *parti-pris*, but also of a sincerity, a living sensibility, a moral earnestness such that I would recommend it to the English reader (and I am sure there are many such) puzzled by the great spirit, the heroic steadfastness that the French have shown in this war, for which he finds little warrant in the 'yellowbacks' on his table. Among many others, this brief record of the mind and conscience of a young

French officer is a *document à l'appui* of no mean value. It relates the story of a youth of twenty who turns from the Radical, humanitarian views of his father, the village schoolmaster, to find salvation (for it is, in his case, really a sort of religious conversion, a change of heart) as a soldier in Africa. And the reader will remark here—as also in the last novels of Emile Nolly—an almost mystical view of military matters recalling the recent German theories.

' " Croyez bien," répondait Nangès, " que la force est toujours du côté du droit."
' L'instituteur se récriait :—
' " Mais certainement," expliquait Timothée. " Qu'est-ce que la force? C'est l'intelligence, la ténacité, c'est la patience, c'est l'habileté, c'est la courage, c'est la volonté. Voilà, Vincent, les facteurs de la force. Voilà les fibres du tissu. Ne croyez-vous pas qu'avec toutes les vertus qui la composent, la force n'a pas de grandes chance d'avoir toujours le droit pour elle?"
' Naturellement, Vincent ne comprenait pas.'
(*L'Appel des Armes*, p. 84.)

Alas, how soon were events to show our young neophyte that intelligence, that tenacity—that patience, ingenuity, courage, force of will—that the most indisputable military qualities may be associated with inhuman, with indeed a devilish perversity! But Ernest did not live long enough to learn all the ripe iniquity of his enemy. He fell

in the very beginning of the war, at Rossignol, on
the frontiers of Luxembourg, midway between
Virton and Montmédy—quite close to Sedan, in
fact; and the Germans thought to make another
great haul there. . . . The fight at Rossignol was
a sort of southern branch of that terrible battle
of Charleroi which no living European can ever
forget. The French Headquarters, perceiving the
ruse and danger of the enemy's plan, set on the
low hill of Rossignol some twelve thousand men,
with orders to hold the heights to the last man
and shield the road beneath where the French
troops were passing in one constant stream; and
the men who died there were not less heroic than
those of Thermopylæ. Twelve thousand, they
were; and I am told that scarce one of them sur-
vived. . . . A few are prisoners of war in Germany.
Picked men, famous regiments, the nearest thing
the French possessed to our time-hardened pro-
fessional soldiers, for they were the Colonial
Infantry and Artillery. The batteries were set
up, and then the storm began. They fought all
day—thirteen hours—against more than a hundred
thousand Germans, holding the passage (one cannot
call it a pass, for the hills there are too low), and,
towards evening, they saw on the horizon a moving
gray mass, and thought for a moment that this
meant reinforcements. Oh, despair! they were
German reinforcements! I say, despair! for such
a feeling indeed fills my breast at reading of this
supreme deception; but the young officer who

gave this account to Psichari's mother, affirms that even then (feeling how useful was the part they played) not despair but a noble exhilaration was the intimate feeling of those heroes on the hill. At last the German army, creeping steadily nearer, and distant now by no more than thirty metres, prepared to take the last irreducible French batteries by assault. At this moment Lieutenant X saw Ernest Psichari lead his Captain, grievously wounded, to the *poste de secours*, immediately returning to face the enemy. He came on with that quick half-racing, half-dancing step which the soldiers call the 'pas gymnastique,' on his face a bright excited smile, and ran with this springing gait to his battery, standing there a moment, still smiling, as he watched the oncoming mass. And then he fell right across his cannon—slipped heavily to the ground; a ball in the temple had shattered that young head, so full of dreams.

'Pourtant, dans sa grande peine, une consolation lui venait. Car il croyait que le sang des martyrs était utile. Sa conviction était que rien n'est perdu dans le monde, que tout se reporte et se retrouve au total; ainsi tous les actes sublimes des héros formaient pour lui une sorte de capital commun dont les intérêts se reversaient obscurément sur des milliers d'âmes inconnues.'

(*L'Appel des Armes*, pp. 295-296.)

And the blood of the martyrs is the seed of Faith.

EMILE NOLLY

No man had welcomed the war with greater
enthusiasm than Captain Détanger : he wrote
under the pseudonym of Emile Nolly. I was not
in Paris on that August morning when he left for
Lorraine, eager (he said) 'to water his horse in
the Rhine.' But I had bidden him good speed a
few years ago, when he set out for Morocco. Shall
I ever forget the transfiguration of that moody,
noble, saturnine face? or the gleam in the great
light-gray eyes, so often sad, or even morose, and
now lit with a wild joy? or the tall, lithe figure-
striding feverishly up and down my little drawing
room while, in a torrent of eloquence, the Captain
tried to explain to my languid feminine imagination (which can only look on, and listen, and gasp
in amazement) 'la joie du combat !' That cam-
paign in Morocco brought him chiefly fatigue and
disappointment, since he and his black troops
had little fighting to do, and were chiefly employed
in convoying from sandy desert to sandy desert
the provisions and munitions needed on the front.
It brought him also, however, the material for a
fine book—a fine, bitter, disenchanted, weary yet
energetic book, eminently characteristic of its
writer—*Gens de Guerre au Maroc.*

One of his three fine books ! It was not those,

however, which brought him the celebrity, almost
the fame, on which he was entering when he fell
in battle. The ardent soul of Détanger had thrown
his talent overboard, as a wandering apostle might
fling from his wallet some useless bauble and go
on unencumbered save by his staff and scrip. His
last two books, the famous ones—*Le Chemin de
la Victoire* and *Le Conquérant*—have indeed little
literary grace and no sort of style; they are like
those varnished Images d'Epinal in cut-out coloured
paper which bring to the humblest cottage a sort
of symbol of the wars of Napoleon, of the glories
of Turenne; or again, like the Stations of the
Cross in some wayside church. They preach a
truth so august, and in the author's eyes so necessary to salvation, that art is of little consequence,
the one thing needful being to make the meaning
plain. That meaning was the same in each : the
saving grace of the Army, and the glorious fact
that any young ne'er-do-well, any weak dilettante
creature even, so he be brave and willing to consent to discipline, may find a personal salvation
there, while building a bulwark of glory round his
country.

I never really ventured to tell Emile Nolly what
I thought of those books, so I said nothing about
them—a language which he perfectly understood
and accepted with that grim, not untender smile
of his. No one better than he knew the charm of
art and romance. And I imagine he felt a certain
fierce pleasure in flinging all that to the winds,

in order, as he thought, to be more useful, reach
a wider public, and influence it with the directness
of a popular sermon. What use, after all, was
there in his two stories of Indo-China, or in *Gens
de Guerre au Maroc*? They were inclined, if anything, to inspire a morbid pessimism. On the
whole, it is the first of his novels which I shall most
often re-read—*Hiên le Maboul*, a book so poignant,
clear and mild in its sadness, that it haunts our
imagination for years after the last page is closed.
No one, perhaps, has so well expressed the peculiar
beauty of Tonquin. . . . When, after Egypt, Aden,
Ceylon, the Frenchman reaches the Delta, his first
instinctive expectation is of something stranger
still; are we not here at the end of the world?

> ' χθονὸς μὲν ἐς τηλουρὸν ἥκομεν πέδον,
> Σκύθην ἐς οἶμον, ἄβατον εἰς ἐρημίαν.'

But what is this gray land where the silvery
winter sunshine floats veiled by an imperceptible
haze? Is it Brittany? Or a misty March day in
the *Landes*, when the sun shines? And see, that
ruined tower set on the round breast of a hill, with
the far-off scaurs and peaks in the background—
is it Auvergne? Nor, in the character of the
conquered people, does there appear at first the
difference that separates the Frenchman from the
solemn Arab or the barbarous Kanak; the Annamite,
with his wide intelligence, his keen and quizzical
wit, his love of hearth and home, his respect for
tradition and his religious indifference, appears at

once a man and a brother. A certain aloofness
adds to his charm. . . . Such was the new and
yet half-familiar world with which Emile Nolly
made us acquainted. *Hiên le Maboul* is a yellow
brother of Loti's *Mon frère Yves*.

And yet, on reopening the charming book (so
appealing in its tender hopelessness, its elegant
sobriety), I find, even here, the Pragmatist apostle
who wrote Nolly's later works ! For what is the
nexus of the novel? It is surely the despair of the
young French lieutenant when he finds himself
impotent to save the native *tirailleur* who, in an
hour of moral anguish, comes to ask his infallible
superior 'les paroles qui guérissent.' Alas, with
all his science, the 'Ancestor with the two stripes'
does not know the words that save; his philosophy
affords him nothing but idle formulas void of faith
and healing. And thenceforth his whole system
of civilisation seems to him wanting and inefficacious.
For Hiên goes out in silence and hangs himself to
a banyan-tree.

Since then Nolly had learned the words that save.
He was, I think, no ardent Catholic, like Psichari
or Péguy; but his faith in the destinies of human
society, his conviction that the army of France
is indeed a Salvation Army, not only for Frenchmen,
but for his dear Senegalese, for black, red, and
yellow—every shade of skin or soul—gave him the
persuasiveness of the men of Napoleon's army.
And he went out into the highways and the by-ways
and compelled them to come in.

And now these young men—so much younger than I, who sit by my lonely fire and remember them—these young men with a future, as it seemed, are all dead for their country and for the faith that was in them. Their bodies lie in wayside tombs, or in the middle of the fields, with a rough cross over them, and a name traced in ink that the autumn rains efface. And that name, which was beginning to shine in the literary record of their nation, that name which they looked to burnish in the course of the next thirty years, can now receive no further lustre. From the personal, individualist point of view, their fame is sacrificed, even as their lives are sacrificed. They are mulcted in their works, as in their race, for, among them all, only Péguy was a father. And, so far as they knew, their immense suffering and sacrifice was in vain. They lie, perhaps, among those dreadful heaps which the shell at once agglomerates and scatters, and from which all individual difference is wiped out. So many of them !

The saddest fate of all, I think, was Emile Nolly's—to die so slowly and so painfully of his wounds, in hospital, while the fight in which he longed to join was raging, still undecided

HENRI BARBUSSE

BEFORE the war, the name of Henri Barbusse was practically unknown. And now he is, of all French writers, the most widely read : he is the Prince of Best-sellers. Bourget has his tens of thousands, his scores of thousands; but *Le Feu* is in its 250th thousand, *L'Enfer* in its 200th thousand, and *Clarté* (published in January, 1919) had reached its fortieth thousand by the beginning of March. And all these novels have appeared in war time, despite the endless difficulties of book-production.

What is the reason of this prodigious success? How is it that Barbusse, who was an unknown young poet in 1913, should satisfy to-day the souls of so vast a public. One may say that he has inherited the immense unsatisfied public left desolate since the death of Zola. He has most of Zola's qualities, imagination; a tragic realism that impresses an image lastingly on the reader's brain; and a sort of public passion, rather than public spirit, that makes him feel other men's grievances and wrongs more keenly than his own. Moreover, he has all Zola's faults—and they are of a kind that do not prejudice the sale of a book—he has Zola's filth, his sexual obsession; Zola's anarchism, and his Utopias; Zola's abuse of horror in the evocation of physical torture.

L'Enfer, M. Barbusse's first great success, is a really bad book! a far worse book, I think, than *Pot-bouille*, with which it invites comparison. Zola showed us an ordinary Paris mansion, or system of 'flats,' and, taking off the roof Asmodeus-wise, revealed on every floor the iniquities it contained, and by so doing the novelist sought to demonstrate the corruption of society in its actual form. His earnestness to some extent redeemed his foulness. And the same holds good of Barbusse. But how miserable is his treatment of the theme. He imagines a respectable boarding-house a kind of Maison Vauquer of a less dilapidated sort. The narrator is one of the boarders. In his wall, a cleft or crevice in a panel puts his bedroom into unsuspected communication with the chamber on the other side. He looks and listens; and what goes on under his spyhole is the unsavoury theme of the volume tersely called : Hell. Debauch, despair, adultery, death, birth; at one moment the consultation of two doctors on a case of cancer; at another, the vigil beside a corpse; such are the things discovered by the peephole of an undreamed-of witness. They are described with a luxury of nastiness which suggests some medical student afflicted with erotomania. He spies upon lust; he prys into the last spasms of pain; his mind is unbalanced. And we imagine him saying to himself, 'Oh, I'll make your flesh creep and your blood run cold !' When he leaves description for theory, he is an Anarchist. Above all, he is a cad, (We are speaking, of course, of the fictitious narrator, and not of M. Henri Barbusse.) But we must admit that he is a gifted and sensitive cad. That is why, although we devote the book to the flames, we read it first. . . .

We have heard how Gautama, brought up until adolescence amid the false enchantments of a sequestered palace, one day crossed the threshold and met, ere he had taken twenty steps, a corpse, a leper, and an old man bent double and blind in his decreptitude : Death—Disease—Old Age—and was told it was the common lot. Whereupon Gautama forsook the world and henceforth his conversation was in Heaven.

M. Barbusse also has met the three spectres, and with them their attendant spirits, Lust and Cruelty. But pity has turned in his heart, not to prayer, but to a passionate anger, a violent reaction against civilisation as it stands. On every page of this first book he shouts 'Follow your instincts ! Eat, drink, and make merry, for to-morrow you die !' And *sotto voce* he seems to add : 'Destroy ! lest ye be destroyed !'

The popularity of Barbusse is therefore a disquieting symptom, but all his novels are not as outrageous as *L'Enfer*. In *Le Feu* he discovered a theme exactly suited to his genius. *Le Feu* is perhaps the only war book which really gives a living image of the war. It is unique and unforgettable. *L'Enfer*, as I have said, is a bad book; but *Le Feu*, with all its faults, is a masterpiece.

It is the journal of a squad—fifteen or a dozen common soldiers in the trenches; their infinite pettiness, their infinite grandeur; the horrors they succumb to or surmount. The first page shows the strange moats or living wells of the trenches —and the strange creatures (huge bears, no doubt) who growl and waddle and stumble therein—'des espèces d'ours qui pataugent et grognent. C'est nous.'

The book is a series of episodes rather than a novel. Strange how this form—which the French call the 'Chest-of-Drawers,' the *roman-à-tiroirs*, comprising a set of independent though sequestered events contained in a solid framework—has taken possession of French literature. M. Duhamel also employs it. *Jean-Christophe* was a *roman-à-tiroirs*. Most popular during the Middle Ages and Renaissance (both the Divine Comedy and Don Quixote are on this model), the Nineteenth Century preferred the firm organic contexture of the novel of character. *La Cousine Bette* or *Madame Bovary*, *The Mill on the Floss*, *Vanity Fair*, *The Old Curiosity Shop*, appeared to us of the Nineteenth Century, a finer development, an evolution. But the world goes round !

Some of these episodes, once read, are fixed in the memory for ever; and of these the finest, I think, is *Le Portique*. Who can forget the death of Poterloo in the explosion of the obus, as he rises from the earth, bolt upright, black, his two arms stretched full length as on a cross, and a flame on his shoulders in place of the shattered head? We cannot banish that terrible image if we would. There are pages of *Le Feu*, which, just glanced at, imprint themselves on our consciousness—like the death of the horse, Trompette, in the mine of *Germinal*, for we are always brought back to our initial comparison of M. Barbusse with Zola. And those who appreciate what I can but call the epic grandeur of *Germinal* or *L'Assomoir*, will do well to read *Le Feu*; while those who cannot endure the foul images, the filthy realism, the coarse slang, the half-mad enthusiasms and indignations of Zola, will be wise in avoiding any book by Henri Barbusse.

For M. Barbusse, like Zola, is an apostle and writes inspired by the energy of his social revolt. Like Péguy—although he is so different from Péguy —he longs to fly to the rescue. There was a medieval saint and poetess, Mechtild of Magdeburg, who sang in one of her lyric prayers, 'O Christ on the Cross, lend me Thine arms to save a suffering world!' That is the prayer of M. Barbusse, only he addresses it to Socialism—or rather, if I understand him aright, to Bolshevism. He would save the dumb dwellers in that dark underworld which, in the present state of things, appears to have no issue. 'And he went down into Hell.' More than once the line has slid into my mind in reading his unedifying pages, and I understood that here, too, was a sort of Gospel—the most modern of the apocrypha.

One may doubt of the wisdom of a social theory which, seeing the stain on our vesture, would simply turn it wrong side out. The stain may go right through. The world may prove no stronger and no saner if you set it upside down. I am not M. Barbusse's political convert. But I admire him for his reaction, his revolt against that which most of us so readily accept—the sufferings of the unknown mass. It is well that there should be writers who rouse and reveal, though their trumpet notes be harsh and unmodulated—well there should be those who shake the sleepers from their sloth and bid them save their neighbours and themselves, building anew, lest the pillars of the temple fall and crush us all in their ruin.

In *Clarté* the ideas of M. Barbusse are explained at full length : abolition of inheritance, universal disarmament, universal equality, universal Republic in the Federation of the World. In this book (which concerns the life of a clerk in the office of a factory, who marries, goes to the war, and returns to look at his wife and society, with not unkindly but disenchanted eyes)—M. Barbusse has lost his coarseness, but also that biting acid which imprinted on our remembrance the scenes of *Le Feu*. In his feminine characters—in the old aunt, in Marie, the wife, in the little blind girl whom every one pities and for whom no one cares—he shows a new quality of tenderness.

What will he give us to-morrow?

GEORGES DUHAMEL

LIKE Henri Barbusse, M. Georges Duhamel has
found his great opportunity in the events of the
war. Before 1914 we knew him as a young writer
of promise in only too many directions. He had
written a play, *A l'Ombre de Statues*, which Antoine
produced at the Odéon Theatre, and which was
(with Marie Lenéru's *Affranchis*) the chief success
of Antoine's heroic voyage of discovery in the
perilous tracts of unknown youthful genius. M.
Duhamel was also just coming into notice as a
poet and especially as a critic of poetry in the
columns of the *Mercure de France*. We liked his
young uncompromising voice and the deliberate
way in which he said that he was proud to be born
in the century which produced a Paul Claudel.
He had as yet published no novel. But the
mobilisation revealed his capacity as a doctor, and
it was as an army-surgeon that he joined the
forces.

His *Vic des Martyrs* (which Mr Heinemann has
published in English as the *New Book of Martyrs*)
revealed a considerable writer, with that rare gift
of insight, of recognition, which pierces at a glance
to the core of things. Tenderness, infinite pity,
regret, a sense of the helplessness of science, a sense
of the hopelessness of so-called progress which ends

in such an explosion of organised disorder—it is these feelings that inspire the good physician as he bends above the murdered youths, the martyrs, whom it is his destiny always to torture and sometimes to cure or to relieve. *La Vie des Martyrs* is a set of brief sketches of the lives and deaths of wounded soldiers in hospital on the front.

With a brief, sure touch (which comes, I think, from his familiarity with the writing of verse), M. Duhamel indicates the few essential outlines which bring into living relief the poor lads to whom he ministers: the Zouave who thought himself so strong when his spine was touched with paralysis; Léglise, of whom his country claimed the double sacrifice of his two legs and who yet found life worth living; Boucheutore—but why enumerate the cases? It is not· the cases that matter, it is the souls that animate these tortured and shattered bodies, which M. Duhamel knows how to make, as it were, transparent to our gaze. There is in these studies (as there was in the eyes of Béal) 'une lumière, une douceur une tristesse extrêmes.' We have heard of the religion of human suffering—and here it wells from a deep and loving nature, full of spiritual richness, and yet totally devoid of mysticism or piety.

I like *La Vie des Martyrs* better than *Civilisation* which followed it in 1918 and was awarded the Prix Goncourt last December. This latter book inclines to the theories of M. Barbusse: Oh, Civilisation, what crimes are committed in thy name!

The setting is the same; the personages are still the wounded soldiers, but also the M.O.'s and great visiting Surgeons, sanitary inspectors, and in these latter sketches M. Duhamel reveals an admirable talent for caricature. There is something of Daumier's biting wit in his portraits of medical 'big-wigs.'

Here is a writer with great gifts, a master of tears and laughter. His sketches are admirable. But has he the gift of organic construction? Will he (as the draughtsman Boz became the painter Dickens) go on from strength to strength?

Time will show.

THE COUNTESS DE NOAILLES

YEARS and years ago—five-and-twenty years ago—
I used sometimes to spend my Thursday afternoons
with a Russian friend; more than once on these
occasions our pleasure was heightened by the musical
talent of her little cousins, the young daughters of
the Princess Brancovan. In my mind's eye I still
see the two children seated on the long piano-stool;
I contemplate their fervent shoulders, their four
thick dark plaits, bobbing from side to side, and
the small eager right hand of one, and the left
hand of her sister, flying up and down the keyboard
as they interpret, four-handed, some difficult page
of Beethoven.

My friend died; years passed; I saw no more of
the young musicians. They grew up; they married.
And then one day, in 1901, a new book of poems
burst—yes, literally *burst*—upon the world of
letters; and I learnt with pleasure and curiosity
that its author, the Countess Mathieu de Noailles,
was the Princess Anna de Brancovan. Like all
Paris, I read her poems.

Have you ever seen, in Switzerland or in Auvergne
(in some mountain country), the spring meadows,
at Eastertime, when the young foals, the lambs,
and especially the little calves (born in the dusk of
the stable in February) make their first irruption
178

into a world of sunshine, of tender and fresh green
grass stretching illimitably in all directions? If
not, and if you would none the less realise the
extreme of joy, of young delight in mere existence,
take down from the shelf *Le Cœur Innombrable*, or
indeed any of the early poems of Madame de
Noailles.

Madame de Noailles resembles no living poet
or poetess. There is none among them who gives
us so absolutely the sense of inspiration—the poet's
frenzy with its flights and its fervours—and also
the flagging, drifting laxness of the verse when
suddenly that inspiration fail. Yet, even in
that wandering delirium, we feel (as in the diviner
poetry of Shelley) no less than the poet's weakness,
the strength and the ardour of the afflatus. On
the frontispiece of her second book (*Les Eblouisse-
ments*, 1907), Mme de Noailles has inscribed a
sentence from Plato's *Banquet* : 'My heart beats
more tumultuously than the pulse of the priests
of Cybele.' And indeed the dance, the extravagant
fury, the κορυβαντιασμός, of the Phrygian festival are
echoed in the strophes of this daughter of Hellas,
married into the house of Noailles. But the young
Mænad (strayed from Parnassus into France) is
never more to my liking than when suddenly she
interrupts her corybantic song to idle in her walled
fruit-garden, making friends with her pears and
apples, praising the brave, bright splashes of red on
the ranks of her scarlet-runners, or counting the
gathered peaches ranged among straw on the shelves

of the fragrant fruitery, while a wasp whizzes out his soul of rage against the dusty window-pane :—

> 'O peuple parfumé des fruits,
> Vous que le chaud été compose
> De cieux bleus et de terre rose,
> Vous, sève dense, sucre mol,
> Nés des jeux de l'air et du sol,
> Vous qui vivez dans une crèche,
> Petits dieux de la paille fraîche,
> Compagnons de l'arrosoir vert.
> Des hottes, des bêches, de fer,
> Gardez-moi dans la douce ronde
> Que forme votre odeur profonde !'

There is in Madame de Noailles something of Pindar—and something of Herrick. I like her best in Herrick's vein, singing the homely things we know with a penetrating, new, and yet familiar sweetness :—

> 'Bien plus que pour Bagdad dont le seul nom
>   étonne,
> Que pour Constantinople, ineffable Houri,
> Je m'émeus quand je vois dans un matin
>   d'automne
> Le clocher de Corbeil ou de Château-Thierry.'

But that other self of hers—the Phrygian pythoness —is no less worthy of our attention. Every page of this volume bears the imprint of her image, ardent, wasted, joyous, excited, full of a mingled asperity and sweetness.   Her voice rings out intoxicated with the wonder of the universe, the mystery of life, the terror of death.   None of the poets of our generation has expressed so keenly the mortal pang caused by the impact of a beauty which is eternal on a system of nerves which is the cobweb of an hour :—

'Je n'ai fait résonner que mes nerfs sur ma lyre.'

It is true there is little of deep emotion and little of pure thought in these earlier poems of Madame de Noailles; but all that the sense can receive of the outer world is exquisitely rendered.   So alive is the poetess to the magic and glory of the visible world that she is jealous of that inner, personal realm which engrosses us so much.   Constantly she regrets those years of childhood, which were objective, calm, free from the tumult of the heart :—

'Enfants, regardez bien toutes les plaines rondes,
    La capucine avec ses abeilles autour,
    Regardez bien l'étang, les champs, avant
        l'amour;—
Car après l'on ne voit plus jamais rien du monde.

'Après l'on ne voit plus que son cœur devant soi,
    On ne voit plus qu'un peu de flamme sur
        sa route,
    On n'entend rien, on ne sait rien, et l'on
        écoute
Les pieds du triste Amour qui court ou qui
    s'assoit.'

But passion is not the only power which contends
with our faculty for absorbing the imperishable
quality of the Cosmos.   There is another, yet more
terrible, which splits the glass in our hands, even
as we raise it to our lips :—

> 'O beauté de toute la terre,
> Visage innombrable des jours,
> Voyez avec quel sombre amour
> Mon cœur en vous se désaltère.

> 'Et pourtant il faudra nous en aller d'ici
> Quitter les jours luisants, les jardins où nous
>   sommes,
> Cesser d'être du sang, des yeux, des mains,
>   des hommes,
> Descendre dans la nuit avec un front noirci.

> 'Descendre par l'étroite, l'horizontale porte,
> Où l'on passe étendu, voilé, silencieux;
> Ne plus jamais vous voir, O Lumière des cieux !
> Hélas ! je n'étais pas faite pour être morte.'

These verses, and many others no less beautiful—
for one of the characteristics of Madame de Noailles
is her abundance—could leave no doubt on my
mind of the quality of the poetess, and I remember
writing, when her second book appeared :—

'There are four lyric poets—there are at least
four lyric poets—writing to-day in France. If we
glance over the land in a sort of bird's eye view,
we see, down by the river, like a faun in the reeds

and rushes, M. Francis Jammes piping on his Pan's pipe a sweet irregular and broken music. His is an elfin spirit, familiar with green things and shy wild animal life; his patrons are St Francis and Ariel. Where the bee sucks, there lurks he; and yet he is not wholly natural. Something quaint, furtive, and precious in his style reminds us of a constant artifice in his simplicity.

'Let us now lift our gaze towards the busier haunts of men; there, in an inspired attitude, stands M. Fernand Gregh, his hand lifted towards the visionary lyre of Victor Hugo, which, like the dagger of Macbeth, hovers before him, just out of reach; yet, though he never wholly grasps it, sometimes the poet snatches a fine strain of music from the strings. A little higher, among the ruins of antiquity, meditates in music M. Henri de Régnier. But who is this who rushes past (her eye in a fine frenzy rolling), singing in an incoherent passion of delight, like the wild shepherdess—*La Ravie de l'Amour de Dieu*—in the Queen of Navarre's delightful pastoral, soaring sunwards in a corybantic ecstasy—who is this lyric muse, half siren and half bird?

" And all a wonder and a wild desire." '

(In those days I had not read the odes of M. Paul Claudel. And, after all, can one call a poet 'lyric,' if he choose to write his rhapsodies in prose?)

A year or two later, our poetess gave us, one after the other, three books in prose—a strange beautiful Oriental prose, charged with colour as the draperies of a Russian ballet, full of a crude barbarian charm. First she produced (I think her best prose book) *La Nouvelle Espérance*.

The novels of Madame de Noailles all tell more or less the same story. They show us a woman of passionate and eager temperament, a soul of suffering ardour, fevered with a sort of avid languor, of fierce tenderness whose cold fit is a sudden revolt of indifference or pride : a woman who reminds us sometimes of Mademoiselle de Lespinasse and sometimes of Phædra ! Need we say that this self-centred and sensual being is unhappy? Yet she is full of poetry, of passion, of charm, half a spoiled child, half an inspired Muse. But she seeks in sentiment and in sensation an Absolute which does not exist on earth. Thus, imprisoned in the tyrannous circle of her own personality, she turns round upon herself, like a squirrel in its cage. So at least we see her in this first novel and in the last : *La Domination*.

Between the two the poetess has placed a sort of pastel, a sort of fairy-tale, exquisite in its refinement and impossible grace, *Le Visage Emerveillé*, where, if the features are the same, the colour and the lighting are so softened that we greet with a smile what, in the other volumes seemed, in all cruel sincerity, the terrible image of hysterical passion.

And then, in the summer of 1913, she produced, after so long a silence of the Muse,

To face p. 184

Photo: Dornac

The Countess de Noailles

her finest poems. Ah! here she is her real self—
she whom Melchior de Voguë used to call, briefly,
emphatically, 'le grand poète,' distinguishing her
thus among her contemporaries. The Countess de
Noailles is really a great poet—the greatest that
the Twentieth Century has as yet produced in
France, perhaps in Europe. In her the romantic
Nineteenth Century has its last echo : her ardent
magnificence, her sense of the wild beauty of natural
things, her lyric cries, her vast horizons magically
evoked, her summits and her tempests, and then
her sudden bursts of simple, friendly homeliness,
recall the genius of Victor Hugo.

But in this new volume the Bacchante, the
Undine, of her earlier poems comes back to us in
tears. Like Prince Gautama when he left his
palace, she has encountered love and sickness and
death. She has learned that to live is to suffer;
she has discovered that man (and especially woman)
has a heart to feel, as well as eyes to see with;
that our destiny is always mysterious and generally
sad. This is no longer the vine-crowned Bacchante,
irresponsible as a young and graceful tiger-cub,
whose sole desire was to satisfy her instinct. This
is not she who, in her tamer moments, tuned her
flute in the sunny kitchen-garden under the warm
south wall, hung with espaliers, smiling as she
sang : 'Yon ripe pear is my heart!'

People will read those earlier poems as long as
they love gardens and the frisky joy of flocks,
and the swift upsoaring flight of the eagle above

the mountain-tops, and all the innumerable many-twinkling smile of Nature. For so I should have called her first volume : not the *Innumerable Heart* (she had not yet grown a heart) but the *Innumerable Smile*, 'αντήριθμον γελασμα. That something mad, and fierce, and glad, and living, can never come again, nor that heroic impatience of mortality —and morality. Our Muse is no longer twenty. Like Thekla she has 'geliebt und gelebet'; she has discovered that inner universe which has no common measure with the material world; she has loved and parted; she has loved and lost; she has looked on the icy face of Death and trembled; she has stood on the pale verge of the unknown abyss.

As we read these lyrics for their splendid music we gradually perceive the motives of the symphony. There is more here than beauty. There is a secret story intricately involved, as in Shakespeare's sonnets or Elizabeth Browning's. The first poems confess the end of a passion, still deep, and quick, but full of quarrels and combats; we feel the inevitable rupture close at hand, and the disenchantment which notes the death of a sentiment that our muse had believed immortal :—

'Te souviens-tu du temps où, les regards tendus
Vers l'espace, ma main entre tes mains gisante,
J'exigeai de régner sur la mer de Lépante,
Dans quelque baie heureuse, aux parfums
    suspendus,
Où l'orgueil et l'amour halcettent confundus?

'A présent, épuisée, immobile ou errante,
J'abdique sans effort le destin qui m'est dû.
Quel faste comblerait une âme indifferente?

'Je n'ai besoin de rien puisque je t'ai perdu.'

The lovers separate. The meeting had seemed a
prodigy. But the Muse, in a cloud of poetry, has
declared to her votaress her jealousy of a mortal
lover :—

'On n'est pas à la fois enivrée et heureuse,
L'univers dans vos bras n'aura pas de rival.'

and the great poet (who has also the misfortune
to be a young and beautiful woman) bids her lover
farewell, much as the immortal Diana may have
dismissed Endymion :—

'Allez vers votre simple et calme destinée;
Et, comme la lueur d'un phare diligent
Suit longtemps sur la mer les barques étonnées,
Je verserai sur vous ma lumière d'argent.'

In vain he protests and begs her to consider how
void and out of shape her days will hang, bereft
of the substance of so rare an affection. A dreary
isolation, a self-centred ambition, are surely less
propitious to poetry than a sympathy communi-
cated, not only between two hearts, but between
two minds? (The man's part of the dialogue we
must more or less supply.) The fact is, she is

tired of him, or rather of the storm and stress of passion, and she replies with an absent look :—

'Je n'avais plus besoin de vous pour vous
    aimer . . .'

'Mon amour, je ne puis t'aimer ! Le jour
    éclate
Comme un blanc incendie, au mont des
    aromates !
Le gazon, telle une eau, fraîchit au fond des
    bois;
Un délire sacré m'emtraîne loin de toi.'

She is relentless, and all the more relentless that she forgets nothing of their old delights. Since Sappho has any woman uttered such a burst of passion as she pours out in shameless reminiscence in the marvellous lyric entitled 'T'aimer. Et quand le jour timide . . .?' (the day may enjoy as much timidity as it pleases; the poetess leaves all her share untouched). Here are the accents of desire, the voice of nature naked and unashamed; but it is the evocation of a love consumed and finished. The remembered flame is now a handful of ashes :—

'O cher pâtre, inquiet et désormais terni,
    J'ai vécu pour cela, qui est déjà fini !

Is there any happiness to equal our anticipation of happiness? Only in listening to music can the

wearied beauty still believe : ‘Qu'il existe un bonheur qui ressemble au désir,’ and then the melody
of Schumann seems to ring with a reproach, a
warning, a presentiment, a final certainty :—

> ‘ Je vois, là-bas, dans l'ombre dépouillée
> Du jardin où le vent d'automne vient gémir,
> Les trahisons, les pleurs, les âmes tenaillées,
> Le vieillesse, la mort, la terre entre-bâillée.’

At this point we lose the clue, and wander a while
in the Pindaric labyrinth of lyrics. A new love,
fresh, kind, and young, appears (we think) on the
horizon. Mindful of her ancient rigours, our muse
hesitates :—

> ‘ Je porte un vague amour, plus grave et plus
>   ancien,
> Qui t'avait précédé et ne peut pas te suivre.’

Yet she does follow her mortal lover. And
again she feels that Nature rejects her, thrusts her,
with a flaming sword, forth from her Paradise
into a disordered world of souls and bodies :—

> ‘Tu n'es plus cette enfant, libre comme la
>   flamme,
> Qui montait comme un jet de bourgeons et
>   d'odeurs.’

This new love is of a different sort, turned towards
eternity, and sometimes, as in the song called *Un*

Abondant Amour and also *Je ne puis pas comprendre,
encore que tu sois né,* we feel that it is perhaps the
love for a child. In any case, her passion is for
some creature still innocent and tender. And this
new feeling—the point of departure for the eternal
life—does really estrange the poetess from her
frenzied pantheism.

> 'Je ne regarde plus
> Avec la même ardeur un monde qui m'a plu.
> Mon esprit tient captifs des oiseaux éternels. . . .
> Je songe au noble éclat des nuits platoniciennes.'

But Fate intervenes to separate the two lovers.
A lyrical intermezzo drags the pageant of a broken
heart through all the miracles of Italy. The universe
has avenged itself upon the woman; she is no
longer the child of the sun, the sister of the winds,
but an unhappy mortal everywhere estranged.
And in this desolation, this fast in the desert,
there dawns upon her the mystic apprehension of
the spiritual world. A series of poems, entitled
Les Élévations, enshrines, this experience of our
eternity :—

> 'Mon Dieu, je ne sais rien, mais je sais que je
>   souffre
> Au delà de l'appui et du secours humain,
> Et puisque tous les ponts sont rompus sur le
>   gouffre,
> Je vous nommerai Dieu, et je vous tends la
>   main. . . .

'Les lumineux climats d'où sont venus mes pères
Ne me préparaient pas à m'approcher de vous,
Mais on est votre enfant dés que l'on désespère
Et quand l'intelligence à plier se résout. . . .

'Comme vous accablez vos préférés, Seigneur
Il semble que votre ample et salubre courage
Veuille assainir en nous quelque obscur marécage,
Tant vous nous arrachez, par des sueurs de sang,
L'âcre ferment vivant, orgueilleux et puissant.
On pense qu'on mourra du mal que vous nous
    faites,
Et puis, c'est tout à coup la fin de la tempête.'

But once again a flaming sword waves before her
eyes and drives her forth from the common experience of humanity; even as Nature and genius
banished her from love, so the cold hand of death
shuts her out from religion. Her beloved dies;
and she has looked on his waxen face, and seen
the leaden coffin go down into the grave.

This terrible moment—which has driven many
in a panic of anguish from the despair of this world
to the desperate hope of a Beyond, as a stag harried
and hunted to the extreme edge of a cliff will
spring into the sea—this 'sombre accident quotidien
de la mort' immures our poetess in the prison of
a stoical grief, where sometimes (but very rarely)
rustle the wings of that angel who led Peter out
of his captivity. In that austere infrangible house
of mourning she remains, aloof from life and Nature,

choosing this living death rather than the treason of a life renewed and fruitful, though bereaved. There she sits still, forgetting the spring and the summer, and looks in a white agony upon the face of Truth. And in verse as firm and full as that of Emily Brontë, she recites the sterile lesson she has learned :—

'Je m'emplis d'une vaste et rude connaissance,
  Que j'acquiers d'heure en heure, ainsi qu'un
      noir trésor,
  Qui me dispense une âpre et totale science;
      Je sais que tu es mort.'

MADAME COLETTE

IMAGINE a young girl in the country, very young, very fresh, sensitive to the finest degree, upright, credulous, and doubtless dainty as a daisy; imagine her in the flower of her youth married and carried off to Paris—to the decadent Paris of the nineties —by a man of the world, who is also a man of letters and a man of science, intelligent, corrupt, and cynical as Mephistopheles himself. No, I am not telling you over again the story of 'Madeleine Jeune femme'; I am telling the history of Madame Colette, and it ends differently.

There is, it seems, an amusement in elaborating the sentimental education of a young bride, in complicating it with excursions into vice and into art; brief, the gifted and immoral author who chooses to be known as 'Willy' was pleased to make over his wife in his own image. She was an artist to the ends of her finger-tips, and they wrote books together—the famous series of *Claudine*— hailed with delight by all that is least strait-laced in Paris (and, in those days especially, there was very little screwing about the moral waist of one sort of Paris!). For Colette Willy realised a personage, always charming to the man about town in its candid perversity, that of the innocent

wanton, or (to quote the title of one of her stories)
L'Ingénue Libertine.

One day I bought one of these Claudine books;
it was called *Claudine en Ménage.* I opened it
and thought it delightful. What an admirable
style, firm and free, full of nature, full of grace.
and the character of the girl, at once shrewd and
naïve, pleased me immensely . . . and then I
began to wonder. . . . And then I did not know
what to do with the book! I would not place it
on my shelf, I could not leave it lying on the table.
Finally, remembering a certain lyric of Robert
Browning's, I took it out into the forest and dropped
it deep in the hollow trunk of a tree. There, among
the pale wood-lice, and the centipedes, and the
fungus, Claudine in her seclusion, finds audience
fit though few.

One day it must have dawned on Madame Colette
Willy that all men were not made on the same
pattern—that there was fresh air somewhere in the
world even for a married woman—that a man might
be a support, and a comfort, and an example—or
perhaps, more simply, that one might do without
one altogether. Anyhow, Madame Colette Willy
became Madame Colette; she divorced her collabor-
ator and began her ascent out of Avernus. She
was, in these new conditions, obliged to earn her
living, and, mindful of the prices paid for even a
successful book, she complicated her profession
as woman of letters with the career of a Variety
Artist.

That is to say, she went on the music hall stage
and was immensely applauded; and I am sure she
is a splendid variety artist—just as I am sure that
Marguerite Audoux must have had a lovely 'cut'
—just as I know (and as any one who goes to the
Place des Vosges can see) that a great cabinet-
maker was spoiled in Victor Hugo. . . . The music
hall feeds its flock. After a few years Madame
Colette returned to literature—returned, I mean,
to the exclusive practice of literature, which she
had never really abandoned—henceforth independent.

A Paris music hall may appear a strange place
of purification, but it all depends on what one is
used to. The courage, the indefatigable industry,
the gentleness, the charity and kindliness of her
new companions impressed Madame Colette; and
she admired the relative pureness of their lives.
We see her, in our fancy (like Roumanille when he
contemplated the lambs frisking in the meadows),
gazing on the clowns, and the quick-change artists,
and the circus-riders, and the dancers, and the
leaders of performing dogs, as she murmurs :—

> 'Coume fan ben tout ço que fan !
> Et l'innoucénço, coum es bello !'

And gradually her novels showed the influence
of a healthier environment. It is true that at first
she wrote *Les Vrilles de la Vigne*. But her last
three volumes possess (with rare literary beauty)

a freedom of soul and a sensitiveness which (at
least, to my thinking, go far to compensate a little
colour-blindness as to morality. Experience has
rendered her wise and sad, indulgent and serene;
it has shown her how to organise her impressions,
so that her art—simple as it is and apparently
facile—has some of the qualities of a philosophy.
In the terms of a metaphor dear to Mr Henry
James, her novels henceforth are, not a slice of
life, but an extract, an elixir.

Not that her last three volumes—*La Vagabonde,
L'Envers du Music Hall*, and *L'Entrave*—are to be
recommended without precaution. They are very
free; they describe a world beyond the precincts
of conventional morality, and they are also very
Pagan. There is mighty little inner life in the
world of Colette Willy! But those who read Mr
Compton Mackenzie or Mr Maxwell will, after all,
find nothing more alarming in *La Vagabonde*, or
even in *L'Entrave*. And they will admire a natural
and yet exquisite faculty of expression—it is difficult
to write with a more delicate exactness than Madame
Colette—and also a psychology, and a sort of disenchanted mansuetude, that go hand in hand with
a love of youth, a sense of youth, quite extraordinary. For my part, I find the lady very taking;
but I do not recommend her to the more serious
admirers of Paul Claudel.

In *La Vagabonde*, we see her as a music hall
star, dropped from the sphere of the woman of
the world, and all the happier in her new orbit,

although aware she is a stranger there. Men, of
course, pay her court, and one of them, Maxime
Dufferein-Chautel (whose tender, bourgeois, authori-
tative nature is admirably depicted) comes very
near to being her lover, and proposes to make her
his wife. But Max, good, solid, faithful, is the least
subtle of lovers—a great, affectionate Newfound-
land dog of a man. And Renée Néré, the vagabond,
who has borne so resentfully the yoke of her first
husband's heart, fears to suffer as much from the
narrowness of a second husband's brain. She cannot
resign her liberty to an inferior, and, on the eve
of their marriage, she sends him a cruel little
letter :—

'Max, mon chéri, je m'en vais,'

and is off with her troupe on a tour to the New
World.

On the first page of *L'Entrave*, she has met
again with this old lover, or rather, herself unrecog-
nised, she has seen him pass, one day at Nice, on
the Promenade des Anglais, he, his young wife, and
his little child. He has not mourned her long !
And Renée feels oddly dispossessed : no one, nothing,
belongs to her; she has no place in the world for
she is no longer a star of the stage. A convenient
inheritance has given her the means of liberty—
that liberty she coveted of old—and she strays
from hotel to hotel on the Riviera mixing with
theatrical visitors, frequenting the better sort

(which, I suppose, means the wealthier sort?) of demi-monde, yet oddly out of place among these amiable barbarians who have neither an idea nor an ideal.

The most barbarian of all is little May, a young hetaira *à la mode*, fresh, fair, and five-and-twenty. Renée is a dozen years older and ought to know better; but she steals poor May's lover away from her; and she shackles herself with this uncultivated young man for life, because she loves him; and it is the first time that she has loved. Ah, she no longer asks herself: is he her equal? . . . Madame Colette, like her heroine, has consented to the hobble, to the shackle, to *L'Entrave*. She, too, has married, has found for herself again a place in organised society, has seen open out before her unsuspected interior horizons, and murmurs perhaps, like Renée Néré :—

'Se peut-il, Beauté, que je te préfère l'âme qui
    t'habite?'

And I await her next novel with almost a tremulous expectation.

MADAME MARCELLE TINAYRE

WHEN Madame Tinayre published her *Maison du Péché*, we thought in France that we had discovered our George Eliot. We pitched our hopes too high; Madame Tinayre is not even a George Sand. But she is a very interesting and gifted novelist. If that first book was of a new and veritable beauty, superior to any which has as yet followed it— but Madame Tinayre is young—it is because the conception of the story entailed a certain simplicity and order of composition, an art of opposition and construction, a severity of style even—in fact, the qualities in which our novelist is generally lacking. Her talent in her subsequent works is no less rich and imaginative; but there is the difference between a rose-tree covered with flowers trained over an espalier, and the same lovely crimson rambler left without support, and dropping half its fragrant burden in the dust.

Madame Tinayre, like most women writers, is endowed with an exact and attentive faculty of observation; like very few women writers, she has a sort of magic, similar to colour or melody, which often disguises the poverty of her compositions; her art aspires to the condition of music; she, too, might say with Saint Hildegard, 'Symphonialis est anima.' She knows how to project, from her

mind into ours, a violent, an incomparable
sentiment, as the waters in the marble fountains of Versailles overlap and drop from one
basin into another.   And she has the culture of
a man.

These are great gifts, sometimes impaired by a
certain warmth and coarseness in the treatment of
love,—an offence rare in male writers, however
libertine, but which hurts our taste occasionally
even in a Mrs Browning (for instance, in *Aurora
Leigh*); and sometimes her fault is a lack of
measure and order which lets her books meander
in a perpetual flux, branching hither and thither,
instead of moulding and rounding them into the
fore-established harmony of a perfect sphere.   In
brief, Madame Tinayre is a romantic.   But just
once, as it were by accident, she consented to the
classic discipline.   And nothing in literature is so
charming, so touching, so delightful, as a romantic
who submits to be a classic.

That 'once' was, of course, when she wrote
La Maison du Péché.   Her art, so often too literal,
and, as it were, photographed from reality without
arrangement (as in the greater part of *La Rebelle*),
at other moments excessive and satiating in its
lyrism, found on that occasion the exact middle
path between experience and imagination.   There
is not only passion in the book and beauty, but
solidity, balance, meditation, reason; there is not
only spontaneity and grace, but a large and firm
knowledge of life, a perspicacity, a sincerity beyond

praise. It has the qualities of poetry and the virtues of prose.

In this novel, Madame Tinayre shows us the clash and the conflict, the attraction and the repulsion, which cause a continual contest between the two halves of France, equally important and irreducibly different. Born into one of these spheres, married into the other, Madame Tinayre is at home in either. Her Augustin, so pure and grave and true, so narrow, so weak, so passionate, is the brother of M. Rolland's Antoinette, is the great-nephew of Pascal. He is a type which has always existed in France, admirable but dangerous, for he is incapable of understanding his contrary. Among French Protestants, Jansenists, strict proverbial Catholics, in certain austere university circles, there are many variations on the type of Augustin. And Fanny, the charming Bohemian, light-hearted Fanny, an artist to the tips of her fingers but only very dimly conscious of being an immortal soul (a pretension which Augustin never abandons for an hour), is not Fanny the very flower of a different, a more frivolous, a lighter, brighter France?

The contact and the conflict of these two natures, their ill-starred, impossible love, is all the story of *La Maison du Péché*: one of the most moving stories of our times. There are readers, there are even critics, who prefer Madame Tinayre's subsequent novel, *La Rebelle*. I have some difficulty, I admit, in catching their point of view. I prefer not only *La Maison du Péché,* but even that exquisite piece of still-life, *François Barbazanges,* which some have condemned on the ground that, though it was art, it was not life. *La Rebelle* is much more life than art. The background, a fresco of popular Paris, is vast, living, and exact; indeed it is too vast, too living, too exact, for it distracts our attention from the rather ordinary characters who occupy the foreground.

And yet there is a great charm in the drawing of Josanne Valentin, the brave young woman-worker married to a neurasthenic invalid—that charm of poignant sincerity which sometimes, in a woman's work, makes the reader's heart beat quicker, as though he had suddenly stumbled on a private confession. Josanne is so courageous, so tender, so kind, that we forgive her conjugal infidelity, and chiefly regret that her lover should be so obviously unworthy of her.

He abandons her—we knew it!—and how pathetic is the scene of their parting—out of doors, in the street, poor Josanne encumbered with the *filet*—the net—in which she is carrying home the materials for the family dinner. That parting scene is unlike any other in fiction in its heart-piercing realism! But Josanne is young, and when the morphino-maniac of a husband (tenderly nursed to the last) departs this life; when Josanne falls in with a high-minded radical philanthropist of the most advanced views, we murmur, much relieved: 'Tout s'arrange.'

For Noël Delysle and Josanne Valentin are alike apostles of a magnanimous democracy: he, a social reformer, author of that notable work, *La Travailleuse*; she, herself a woman-worker, the feminist reporter of a ladies' newspaper, in constant contact with the poor in need of help, and the fevered, fussy world of philanthropy. Self-subsisting, 'generous' in the wide sense which Descartes gives to the word, Noël Delysle and Josanne Valentin alike reject the tyrannous old dictum of Arnolphe :—

'Bien qu'on soit deux moitiés de la société
Ces deux moitiés pourtant n'ont pas d'égalité.'

For them, the woman-worker, self-supporting, independent, has attained a moral and social equality with man, and should be judged by the standard of what Mr Shaw, we believe, has called the New Morality.

They both possess that 'vraie générosité' which consists in self-reliance, strength of will, endurance, contempt for opinion, and respect for the liberty of others. Descartes thought nothing more useful than to foster a race of such generous individuals, 'sachant subsister par soi-même . . . pour ce qu'ils n'estiment rien de plus grand que de faire du bien aux autres et de mépriser son propre intérêt.' And, despite one secret blemish in her past, Josanne feels herself a member of this *élite*, a factor of progress. Nor does she attach any great importance

to a back-sliding which is not esteemed too damn-
able by the men and the women of the New
Morality. She makes her confession to Noël
Delysle in much the same spirit as Tess of the
D'Urbervilles unbosoms herself to Angel Clare.

For reformers are prompt to forget that what
was human nature in the past, what may be human
nature in the future (should they and others persist
in their modern ideal), is not human nature *now*.
The mind of man has modified all things around
him and within. From the seeding-grasses in the
hay he has produced the varieties of corn; from
the small and acid crab-fruit in the hedge, the
rennet and the Ribston pippin; and from the poison-
ous roots of foreign forests our daily domestic
potato. Our morality is another product; we may
modify it yet further; such as it is, at present it
remains our staff of life. And the staunchest
feminist in the world, if he be a man and in love,
will expect his wife to be tender, chaste, and
faithful, and care little enough whether or no she
be self-reliant, generous, and brave.

Noël Delysle is a stronger man than Angel
Clare, and proportionately less hard and dour;
but he receives the shock of Josanne's confession
with little less dismay. He learns then that the
little stepson who will share their home—the child,
he imagined naturally, of the unfortunate Valentin
—is in reality the son of Josanne's lover. In
treating such a situation, Madame Tinayre is at
her best. The central fact of all her novels is the

struggle between nature and nurture, between instinct and convention. Deep, deep below the intellectual superstructure, the primitive man, the primitive woman, stir in her heroes. His virtues and tolerances fall from Noël Delysle, leaving him jealous and passionate; her valour and self-reliance fade in Madame Valentin, and Josanne, the rebel, becomes the merest woman.

La Rebelle is an interesting book, but how much do I prefer (though its faults lie thick upon it) *L'Ombre de l'Amour!* [1] The tale rambles on as it pleases, independent of design or composition, poorly constructed enough with its two long parallel lines, as monotonous, if as impressive, as those low, even cliffs which enclose between their grassy walls some Limousin or Gascon valley.

Bis repetita placent is a good motto if we wish to amuse; for (as Bergson has pointed out) there is something comic in reiteration, in a repeated misadventure, and especially in a double fall— every clown knows that! In spite of the rare beauty and sincerity of the character-drawing, this tale of two pure girls stumbling, one after the other, in the same secret slip, does produce an effect of painful ludicrousness.

The defilement of a young girl in her innocence is the most pathetic of themes, but it is its singularity alone that makes it touching. Mephistopheles, in his cleverness, degrades the misery of poor Gretchen when he observes: 'Sie ist nicht die

[1] Translated into English under the title: *The Shadow of Love.*

Erste.' We must imagine no angel ever tripped before; we must have very present in our sight the state of innocence from which she is thrust out. So the wise Walter Scott places beside his sad Effie the peerless Jeanie Deans. So George Eliot relieves the abasement of Hetty by the pure brilliance of Dinah. But in this novel of Madame Tinayre's, there are but two young girls, and, by an inconceivable error, she involves them both in the same miserable mystery. Involuntarily we protest. I, for my part, protested, and the novelist replied :—

'Il me semble que votre principale objection porte sur le double effet d'une double aventure, qui vous paraît un artifice littéraire. Mais, dans ma pensée, il fallait que Fortunade complétât Denise, que la pitié spirituelle pour le maudit aboutit au même échec que la pitié plus physique pour le malade. Fortunade, c'est, en tout petit, Eloa. Je crois que ces 'doubles' ne sont pas sans exemples dans les grandes œuvres de la littérature, et que de glorieux précédents auraient pu m'enhardir, si j'avais hésité. Dans la réalité même on voit des âmes de même nature se deviner et se rapprocher.'

The literary doubles of which our author speaks are a charming device when the novelist treats of what is normal, salutary, or pleasant : we love to see Rosalind by the side of Celia, or the Two Gentlemen of Verona; but we should not care to look at two Quilps, or two Deformed Transformed,

or two Gretchens, or even two dumb girls of Portici.
The abnormal does not suffer repetition.

So I persist in my protestation, and all the more
because I love and admire the two sweet girls, so
pure, so devoted; ruined and debased, the one by
pity for a man's bodily sufferings, the other by
compassion for his moral state. For Madame
Tinayre, following the theories of Spinoza and
Nietzsche, looks on pity as a debilitating emotion,
relaxing the fibres of the soul and predisposing to
an ignoble self-surrender.

But how charming is the first half of this novel;
the opening scene in the country doctor's dining-
room, with the two girls seated in the red-paved
parlour that smells of damp bricks and freshly-
washed linen and ripe apples. Denise, the young
lady of the house, is the soul of a home :—

> 'A perfect woman, nobly planned
>   To warn, to comfort, and command——'

a large human type, as easily imagined in England
or Scotland as in Central France. But the girl
who sews at her side is essentially Limousine, her
very name, Fortunade, recalls the pathetic head
of the girl-saint of the Corrèze whom she resembles
—pensive and slim, with the pursed, plaintive
mouth, the suffering grace of her profile, and the
something dreamy, sweet, yet almost sullen that
makes her appear half a Gothic angel and half a
scolded child.

Fortunade Brandou is only a little peasant, the daughter of the village innkeeper, who goes out sewing by the day to the few gentlemen's houses in the countryside. But all the dreams, all the visions, all the missionary fervours and superstitious fears of a Celtic race are locked beneath the smooth black braids of her roundly projecting brow. Her longing is not to be happy, but to expiate, to redeem, to fly to the rescue of the oppressed. She must up and grapple with sin and sorrow. She cannot let the evil-doer perish before her eyes. Fortunade, with her feeble body full of suffering grace, her doleful smile, her plaintive voice, has the soul of Corneille's Pauline, destroying the idols of the Temple and braving the Proconsul; has the faith and the fervour of a Joan of Arc, letting slip her shepherd's crook to grasp an enchanted sword.

And, even as she must suffer and struggle for the moral welfare of her fellow-mortals, so Dr Cayrol must needs overcome and stamp out disease. Each of these personages is a type—complete, rare, and living—animated with an extraordinary racial truth. In describing the peasants and the mountain of Corrèze, Madame Tinayre puts us in contact with her own familiar country. There are few more beautiful in France as scenery; none more noble as a focus of human character.

Those who have studied the deep wave of moral feeling which broke over France between the fall of the First and the rise of the Second Empire—

students of the Saint-Simonians, historians of '48
—have always been struck by the great proportion
of men from the southern centre—from Auvergne
and Corrèze—generous, philanthropic, active sons
of Utopia, brusque and kind, avid for justice as
the prophets of Israel. These minds, less intellectually or theoretically great than large and magnanimous, form one of the finest categories of the French
character.

In no novel have we come across so adequate a
presentment of them as in the village doctor—
worthy *confrère* of Mrs Gaskell's country surgeon
and of Balzac's *médecin de campagne*—the rustic
savant, interested in the scientific and social movement of his times yet homely in his private tastes
and standards of life; parsimonious in pence,
and liberal with his rare gold pieces; distrustful
of all strangers, yet quick to harbour a fresh chimera;
prompt to anger; to all appearance just a son of
the soil, a hearty meat-fed man, fond of his glass,
fond of his pipe, fond of his gun, striding at ease
in his strong solid shoes and his old country clothes
—but a sage for all that, and nearly a saint; a
man, at least, in the best sense of the word, with
the root of the matter in him. Such a man, choleric,
proud, and kind, is Étienne Cayrol, at once the
hero and the father of the heroine in *L'Ombre de
l'Amour*.

We recognise him at once and love him from
his very entrance on the twelfth page, when he
comes in, out of the mud, and the dark, whistling

the air of a country reel, and greeting, with kind, quizzical observant eyes, the two young girls mending the linen in his parlour.

'Il avait un visage de vieux chef gaulois, coloré, couperosé aux pommettes, les cheveux gris, l'œil bleu saillant, le nez aquillin, la mâchoire solide sous une longue moustache dédorée. Comme il inclinait la tête, on voyait l'attache puissante du cou, et cette forme du crâne qui s'unit à la nuque par une ligne droite, caractéristique chez les gens du Plateau central. Les épaules étaient carrées, le torse trapu; les jambes un peu arquées devaient peser lourd sur le sol. Toute la personne—sans finesse mais non pas sans noblesse—d'Étienne Cayrol, révélait l'origine paysanne. Elle exprimait la force, une force stable, lente, réfléchie, sûre d'elle même.'

And yet (an observation admirably in accordance with the history of the type) some secret defect of judgment condemns the dearest schemes of the doctor (so well considered, so unselfish in their working out, so noble and yet practical in their aim), but destined none the less, to miscarry and 'gang aft agley.' His unfinished sanatorium scars the hill-top with the mean unsightly ruins of uncompleted work; and the consumptive youth, whom he takes into his own home to nurse back to health, not only dies, but seduces the doctor's only daughter: the girl who was the pride of his heart, as the sanatorium was the dream of his mind.

Denise Cayrol is a noble creature, strong, kind, and pure. At twenty-seven years of age she no longer thinks of herself as a young girl; she is not concerned with love and marriage, and it is rather with a half-maternal, half-sisterly devotion that she tends the young consumptive, a few years younger than herself, who is so eager to live, so ardent in loving, and whom her clear, reasonable judgment and pitiful heart see from the first as marked with the signs of his doom. Denise attracts the hapless Jean with all the force and promise of her health. When the doctor suspects the secret engagement that binds his daughter to his patient, he is both jealous and indignant (for he cannot conceive how a woman can love a consumptive), and he sends Jean away into a sanatorium. But Jean falls ill; Denise rushes to his death-bed, and then and there (in a wild pitiful desire to pour out all the best of life, in one moment, while there is time) she yields to his fevered desire; she succumbs.

There were two girls seated in the red-paved parlour, that smelt of damp bricks and freshly-washed linen and ripe apples, when the doctor strode in from the dark night outside, on the winterly evening which opens the novel. The second is Fortunade Brandou, the little village dressmaker, the mystic; an ill-judged pity lures her, too, to her undoing. When Veydrenne, the poacher, the

outlaw, breaks his leg, Fortunade tends the village
miscreant in his illness and strives to save his
soul :—

'Ce serait si beau de sauver cette âme !'

Alas, when did the wolf listen to the voice of
Little Red Riding Hood? The sweet, the mystical,
the charitable Fortunade fell prey to a wild beast,
and the deep gorges of the mountain torrent
received the soiled, childish body that dared no
longer affront the light of the sun.

'Morte, morte ! non par le hasard d'un faux pas,
non par un chagrin d'amour, elle n'avait jamais
aimé que Dieu, la chaste fille : Dieu et ses pauvres !
morte pour être allée vers celui que tous haïssaient;
morte pour avoir tenté l'enterprise folle de sauver
une âme perdue ! . . . Perdue elle-même sans doute,
brutalement outragée, deux fois victime, elle
avait payé de sa pudeur et de sa vie l'imprudence
sublime de sa pitié.'

These characters are conceived with the sure
and intimate reality that comes of kinship; we
feel that Madame Tinayre is of their race and their
habitation. Here, her foot is on her native heath,
and she compels our interest far more powerfully
than when she writes of Paris (her Paris is always
a little too 'Rive gauche'); when she pictures her
Corrèze, when she evokes the mountain scenery

round Brives or Tulle, I think no French novelist since George Sand has possessed so masterly a touch in peopling a living landscape with living beings. Indeed, remembering the pastoral novels of Our Lady of Nohant, recalling 'Marie Claire,' comparing them and this book of Madame Tinayre's with *The Mill on the Floss* and *Adam Bede*, it seems to me possible that one of the greatest gifts of woman as a novelist may lie in her singular power of rendering country life in all the variety of its personages, its customs, and its natural background.

MLLE MARIE LENÉRU

A LINE from one of the essays of Suarès might serve as a motto for all the plays of Mlle Lenéru : 'La conscience malade, voilà le théâtre de la fatalité moderne.' A sick conscience, a soul diseased —in other words, the problem of evil; or, in more modern phrase, the war between an over-developed personality and the rights of others; such is the theme which her genius, at once lucid and sombre, ardent and logical, treats with a penetrating passion, with almost, as it were, a sort of introspection, as though, in face of some grave derogation from current morality, she had said : How did a nature, apparently excellent, arrive at such a pass? How should I, in his place, have fallen and yet have remained consequent with all that I was up to the moment of failure? So that the dramas of Mlle Lenéru have the gravity and the spiritual ardour of an examination of conscience. They seem to radiate from an inner self full of revolt, passion, and implacable reason.

Not that Mlle Lenéru is religious. In writing this little book, it is borne in upon me very clearly that man, not woman, is really the religious animal. But Mlle Lenéru is not the usual free-thinker ; she is, so to speak, a theologian turned inside out. There is about her something of the unfrocked priest who, whatever his present opinions, feels himself always a priest, entrusted with the souls of others and responsible for their eternal fate. She no longer accepts the promises and the commandments of revealed religion; but nothing else appears to her of really great importance.

In all she writes we recognise the conflict of a proud and ardent character, a passionate and avid sensibility, with a soul enamoured of honour, order, discipline, self-immolation; so that we never know which is the real Marie Lenéru : the impassioned anarchist convinced that the one important thing in life is for each individual to become the most perfect example possible of his own peculiar type; or the ascetic, eager to sacrifice the visible and natural life to a life invisible and supernatural.

It is this double nature, doubtless, which gives so much substance to the plays of this young writer. She conceals in her heart a romantic who died young—or rather he is not dead, only buried in a perpetual *in pace*, whence his voice sometimes issues in revolt or appeal; but her mind is given over to the rule of a bitter and splendid reason which assures her that neither the State, nor the family, nor any constituted form of society, based on a firm tradition, needs genius so much as order, passion so much as discipline, grandeur so much as happiness; and indeed in all her plays she sacrifices (as Brutus sacrificed his sons) the first of these catagories to the second.

Her sensibility remains imbued with those ideals

of individualism and ambition which reigned in France throughout the nineties : she was born under the Consulate of Nietzsche and of Ibsen; but experience and reflection have shown her the disasters of a moral anarchy which still engages her sympathy though she augurs no happy issue for it. On the frontispiece of her first book, *Les Affranchis*, she has written a couplet from Racine's *Titus et Bérénice*, expressing this antagonism between the individual and his environment : two lines in which the Jewish Queen, sacrificed by her royal lover to reasons of state (*invitus invitam*), reminds him of his duty to himself—and to her :—

'Rome a ses droits, Seigneur, n'avez-vous pas
    les vôtres?
Ses intérêts sont-ils plus sacrés que les nôtres?'

And this question resumes a theme which never ceases to occupy her tragic sense of passion and her strong intellectual curiosity.

Her first play is the history of a grand passion in two undisciplined yet superior natures—two super-mortals—despite society, and law, and order. Philippe and Hélène are (as Gobineau would say) 'Children of the King,' morally and intellectually a head and shoulders above the people. By what process of reflection are they induced to sacrifice a miraculous possibility of happiness, a draught such as they alone might quaff, to rights and duties which they do not acknowledge? Why, being giants, do they submit to the bonds of the pygmies? Are they right, are they wrong in the renunciation? Is there only *one* right and *one* wrong? Such are the questions raised by the history of her *Affranchis*—her Free Souls, thus most ironically named, since, in fact, none of us is free, and we act, not as we would, nor as we should, but as we can.

Philippe Alquier is a philosopher, a great professor, a pioneer of ideas, an idol of the young : in fact, a sort of Bergson, a sort of Barrès—the Barrès of yesterday. He believes neither in duty, nor in the moral law, nor in any Absolute, nor in any certitude; and he discerns, in the floating relativity of things, but one obligation, that of augmenting to its utmost his personality. He is married to a pleasant, pretty wife, whose irritating mediocrity is, so to speak, the hall-mark of her virtue : it is impossible to be more respectable than Marthe. In the early Twentieth Century, at the dissolution of French monasteries, Alquier, the philosophic anarchist, receives under his roof his wife's sister, Mother-General of the order of Reformed Cistercians, Abbess of Fontevrault.

Under his roof—or rather under *her* roof, for the Abbess of Fontevrault is co-heiress with her married sister in the properties which the Alquiers inhabit, both in Paris and in the country. But necessity in this case is doubled by no disapprobation : Philippe Alquier naturally believes in the rights of minorities. Although politically of the

extreme left, he would in this affair have voted
with the extreme right (as did many Dreyfusards
some twenty years ago, who opposed the banish-
ment of their political enemies, the Jesuits), and
thus, in the opening scene, the author establishes
her hero's refusal to allow the tyranny of the
greatest number.

The abbess brings with her a postulate of her
order, secularised like herself, but (in the case of
the girl) before she had pronounced her vows.
Hélène Schlumberger, young, beautiful, intelligent,
and rich, is naturally the heroine of the piece. Her
mind, the fresher that hitherto it has been restricted
to the skyey sphere of theology and ethics, revels
in the wide and indiscriminate culture with which
Alquier delights to enrich it. Nietzsche, Bergson,
Anatole France, she absorbs all without a protest.
Naturally, history repeats itself, and Abelard falls
in love with Héloïse, and Héloïse still deeper in
love with Abelard.

What, in this conjuncture, is the duty of a free
soul? Shall Philippe Alquier divorce his faithful,
admirable, uninspiring wife? Shall he keep a
virtuous young lady as his secret mistress? He
makes both these proposals, but he makes them
as one who feels how impossible they are. For we
act, not in accordance with what we actually think
and believe, but as persons still inspired by what
we used to think and have long been in the habit
of believing : when Alquier proposes a divorce to
the girl he has educated in the ideas of Nietzsche,

her first instinctive cry is : *Et les autres ?* She is
an altruist still, and a Christian, in spite of herself,
and acts according to an impetus given years ago,
perhaps before her birth.

Hélène in the convent to which, unbelieving,
she retires, is happier, probably, than she would
have been as Alquier's concubine (setting society
at defiance) or as his wife, Hagar enthroned, having
sent out the lawful Sarah into the wilderness. In
the convent at least she finds, if not a faith, a rule
of life. A discipline and an ideal are things more
intimately necessary to her soul, such as the ages
have formed it, than the happiest passion, if
satisfied in their despite. And Alquier, too, will
acquiesce. When he threatens the abbess with
political reprisals, with the ruin of her order, she
smiles :—

'Vous ne ferez rien de tout cela, Philippe, et
vous me donnerez votre fille à élever.'

In her second play, *Le Redoubtable* (produced at
the Odéon Theatre in January, 1912, and with-
drawn by the author after three representations),
Mlle Lenéru shows still more forcibly the monstrous,
the almost cancerous growth that a too exasperated
personality may become in an organised community
of mediocrities.

Georges Malte is the most brilliant naval officer
of his promotion; all that an individuality can
acquire and possess in one generation, he has

acquired, he possesses. But nothing else, neither traditions, nor inherited breeding, nor the instincts of a gentleman, nor even fortune; Malte is the son of an Italian pastrycook, and no more French by birth than Napoleon, or Zola, or Gambetta—who, after all, were pretty tolerable Frenchmen. And his soul is devoured with ambition for the refinements he does not inherit; and his mind is consumed by the desire to be first, by that *amor dominandi* which is, in certain natures, the strongest passion of all.

And his heart is wholly occupied by the mistress he adores, who is, most simply and most naturally, all that he can never be : the child of a ruling race. Laurence Villaret is the daughter of one admiral, the wife of another. For six years she and her lover have belonged to each other in secret, and at length the time comes when Malte (who in his love of supremacy has affected the rich man) feels his creditors close upon him and disgrace near at hand. Money he must have or farewell to his career, good-bye to the love of his life.

Unfortunately, a brilliant officer has always at his disposal one means of raising funds—if he listen to temptation. And Malte listens. He communicates to a foreign power certain secrets, and the good ship *Redoubtable* is rendered worthless— just as the *Affranchis* were not free; just as *La Triomphatrice* will be shown to be an unloved, broken-hearted, solitary woman. All Mlle Lenéru's titles are epigrams of irony ! Yet, in *Le Redoubtable*.

Mlle Lenéru has given us the *reductio ad absurdum* of her former theme. If, at the close of the *Affranchis*, we doubted whether the lovers were wise in sacrificing their utmost joy 'au bon gouvernement du monde' (and such is the contagious force of passion that we had left the theatre happier after seeing them elope to some undreamed of isle), we doubt no longer when we have seen *Le Redoutable*.

Although we may admit that the moral law is in process of evolution, though we may look forward to a day when a new vital order shall supplant our established order, yet, meanwhile, we must observe the rules of the game, even though they mean no more to us than the rules of a game ! In fact, however we choose to *think*, there is but one profitable way of *living* : that which consists in treating as fundamentally true those truths alone which have weathered the experience of generations. *Foris ut moris, intus ut libet.* Or as Pascal puts it : 'Il faut dire comme les autres, mais ne pas penser comme eux.'

And so Mlle Lenéru, one of the rare individualists of the younger generation, Mlle Lenéru, so romantic, with her love for the noble, the exceptional, with her revolt against platitude and mediocrity, repeats, in a mood of revolt and irony, the refrain of Jules Romains :—

'Nous cessons d'être nous pour que la Ville dise :
  MOI !'

This young writer, so extraordinary by reason of her depth of meditation, and the strange Pascalian vigour and beauty of her language, was the more surprising (and yet perhaps the more explicable) because of a singular infirmity : she lived immured in an interior world. If, indeed, her short-sighted vision perceived a vague image of our earth and its inhabitants, the noisiest city left her undisturbed to her reflections. Mlle Lenéru was absolutely deaf. She heard no echo of the applause which greeted the *Affranchis*. In 1918 when the comedians of the Théâtre Français read and accepted 'à l'unanimité,' her new play, *La Triomphatrice*, she alone remained unmoved. The blindness of Milton, the paralysis of Heine, the deafness of Beethoven, have accustomed us to these ironies, or compensations, of a mysterious fate.

The humble ferment which produces alcohol when its development is checked and interrupted, flourishes as an unproductive mildew if its organism find all that it requires. An obstacle is often the stimulus of genius. But when genius has made at last a pearl of the wound, a ruby of the fissure, and turned starvation into rapture, how cruel appears the sudden fate that snatches the hard-earned prize from its grasp ! Marie Lenéru died of the grippe on the 23rd of September, 1918.

THE PASTORAL NOVEL

THERE has always been a pastoral novel in France, because France is an agricultural country. Except milk, meat, and a little bread, England draws too little of her nourishment from her own resources; her plenty is a cheap import; and even the beauty of much of her landscape suggests an indifference to agriculture. We have known a French admirer, confronted with a marvellous panorama of wild Sussex heath—wood, grassy links, and gorse-covered common—contemplate the scene and sigh, 'Rien, rien, rien, à se mettre sous la dent !'

France, on the other hand, is self-sufficing, almost self-supporting, and always has been so. If we consider the Duke of Berry's *Book of Hours* we realise that in many parts of France the business of life has continued almost unchanged since the Fourteenth Century. From the pruning of the vine in February (our month of March) to the fattening of the swine in the oakwoods in November, while the wood-cutters mark the trees for felling, here are just such scenes as the dweller in rural France has constantly before his eyes to-day, unaltered —scenes which the accumulated associations of countless generations have invested with a human interest more poignant, more intimate, than any which mere landscape can afford. And we admire

223

the French peasant; his frugality, his industry, his endurance are indeed beyond all praise; his economy is marvellous, and such is his good humour that he makes a pleasure of his self-denial; miserably lodged, poorly fed, he is conscious of no inferiority; he knows himself to be the backbone of France.

The peasant and the landscape for ages have remained unchanged. France is so large a country, with so great a variety of soil and climate, that there are all sorts of French peasants : materialistic, clean, bright, and gay, in Touraine and the Charentes; superstitious, poverty-stricken, imaginative, in Vendée and Brittany; good-humoured, ambitious, and positive in Auvergne—and so on through all the nations of France. When you knew the place, you knew the peasant—until quite lately. The 'regionalist' (the provincial) novel has come into being just when the field labourer himself has ceased to be regionalist, or provincial; for military service is a wonderful leveller and unifier.

Until the middle of the last century (until, that is to say, the days of George Eliot in England and the latter days of George Sand in France), a Fourteenth-Century peasant might have revisited his country parish almost anywhere in France, and have noted little alteration to mark the flight of time. The last fifty years have made more difference in rural matters than the five centuries that went before them. The dairy farms of Normandy with their patent separators, their ferments for

cheese flavours, sent down in neat little tubes
from the Pasteur Institute; the arable lands with
their great red, throbbing mechanical sowers,
reapers, binders, automatic ploughs, threshing
machines, etc.; the network of roads with their
motor-cars and bicycles; the train whirling past
in a white puff of smoke behind the screen of poplars;
such homely sights of our everyday Twentieth
Century would cause a mediæval husbandman to
open his eyes considerably.

He would have to seek the depths of Brittany,
the heart of the Cantal, the wastes of the Lozère,
to find some faint image of the world he knew.
There, indeed, save for the frequent crops of
potatoes and buckwheat, which he would not
recognise, he would find little changed; the one-
toothed wooden plough still scores its furrow on
the steep hillside; the thud of the flails is loud in
the dusk of autumn evenings; in the fields the
women stoop and gather the buckwheat into
stooks and bind it standing, even as the reapers
cut the stalks from the ground; the old pastoral
life continues, not greatly changed for better or
for worse. But even here the century-old country
life of France is menaced, and that threat hanging
over it renders it more dear, and almost sacred,
that the rural novel in France is at once more
exact and more tender in its record than it was
in the century gone by.

When I came to live in France in 1888, there
was a pastoral novel of course—there has always

been a pastoral novel in France, as I said—but it was of a most calumniatory and reviling sort. Great was my surprise, when I spent my summers in the country, to find that the old gaffers on the farms were *not* left to die of hunger and neglect when they could no longer work, but, on the other hand, were treated with the utmost honour and consideration, given invariably the best seat on the settle, the best wine, expensive tonics from the doctor's shop, and all that filial kindness could devise. Maupassant's wonderful stories, Zola's *La Terre*, must evidently have some foundation in fact. But my personal experience has not corroborated their pessimism.

Then, after the pastoral novel *genre rosse*, came, with the very last years of the Nineteenth Century, the reign of the social novel; and, as a matter of course, the pastoral novel followed suit. The best stories of those times, I think, are René Bazin's, especially that most picturesque and touching idyll of a farm in Vendée gradually destroyed by the rural exodus, *La Terre qui Meurt*. In *Donatienne*, the same writer paints the poverty of a Breton village, and the temptation—almost the dire necessity—which induces the young mother to quit home and children in order to earn the large wages, and live the facile days of a wet-nurse in Paris. And, naturally, he shows the moral (and finally the material) ruin which follow on that ill-judged step.

In *Le Blé qui Lève* (The Growing Corn), René

Bazin describes the life of the woodland labourers —the foresters, wood-cutters, charcoal-burners, and so on—who form an important part of the rural population in France; and he shows them ravaged by strikes, syndicates, etc.; for M. Bazin is nothing if not Catholic and Conservative.

Yet the tone of his novels—though in my brief account the stories sound melancholy enough—is as far removed as possible from the *roman rosse* of the Eighties; M. Bazin is full of faith and hope and charity; he is, in spite of human malice, so convinced of the final triumph of God that we might write on all his books the refrain of Æschylus :—

'Sing alas ! and say alas ! But the Good shall
  come to its own !'

Αιλινον, Αἰλινον ειπε, το δ'ἐυ νικατω.

In those last years of the Nineteenth—in those first years of the Twentieth—Century, while René Bazin's angelic voice was welling up in treble ecstasies, the pastoral novel in France had other notes which held, as it were, the bass—deep, strange notes—brief, complicated, syncopated phrasing. In other words, Jules Renard and Charles-Louis Philippe were giving their sense, too, of the life of woods and fields.

I wrote once that Jules Renard was the Hokusaï of French literature. He just glances at an object, sees its essential character, fixes that and neglects the rest; a bird, a flower, a little boy with carroty

hair and sensitive, eager eyes, a scolding house-
wife, best of all, perhaps, an old, old country-woman,
who cannot read or write, but who is full of the
knowledge of things. I would give even *Poil-de-
Carotte* for *Ragotte*! The quarrel of Ragotte and
her son, 'le Paul,' moistens one's eyes with the
tenderest pity; and yet it is told with a dry, almost
a hard precision, a concise sobriety; not a word
superfluous. The thing happened so, and a pity
'tis 'twas so; there's no more to be said. But
underneath this real compassion there is a sad
certitude of the end of all things, a melancholy
nihilism, a hopeless irony.

Few books are sadder reading than Jules Renard's
Bucolics. This harsh, terse, impassible writer
breaks our heart by his choice of a subject : an
ill-treated child, a helpless, infirm old woman. If
we smile at anything that he evokes, it is seldom
a happy thought, a hopeful suggestion, but some
quaint image or touch of character, for Jules Renard
enjoyed the gift of an incomparable visual imagination : he makes us see the bushy-tailed squirrel
flitting through the autumn woods and lighting
up all the dead leaves with his bright brush as he
passes; or old Mother La Chalude, knitting as she
walks, who has threaded on her apron string the
pierced kernel of an apricot and placed it at her
waist, a little to the left, to support the end of
one of her knitting needles; or older Honorine,
coming across the field-path, bent double, so that
she appears a headless woman, while her stick,

on which her rugged hands stand out like knots,
is higher than her cap.

This keen appreciation of the beauty and
character of Nature, combined with a tragic sense
of the aimlessness and incertitude of human destiny,
are the peculiar quality, I think, of the closing
Nineteenth Century: a mingling of enchant-
ment and disenchantment. Nowhere, of course, is
it so remarkable as in Pierre Loti, but he is out of
our perspective—which only concerns the Twentieth
Century. We have noticed it in Jules Renard, only
lately dead (1864-1909). We shall find it again, with
less artistry and a more poignant pity, in another
writer, ten years younger, who died about the
same time, Charles-Louis Philippe; as we found it
in Madame Colette.

Jules Renard was one of the rare French authors
of our time who do not scorn to love their calling;
who are men of letters from the bottom of their
soul, and not principally apostles, or disciples, or
reformers, or philosophers;—who are as happy as
Flaubert when at last they enclose an aspect of
reality, however humble, in some perfect phrase
as pure as the amber which preserves a fly. Renard
had ideas and passionate convictions of his own;
to resume, let us say that they were the exact
opposite of the ideas and passionate convictions
of a Paul Claudel; but he did not usually write
to express or to expound his peculiar theory of anti-
clericalism or democracy. If these opinions came
into the picture, he noted them with his customary

poignant exactitude, no more. Only once did he think of writing a play with a purpose. His great, his scrupulous endeavour was to represent reality as he saw it, just as it struck his shrewd, short-sighted gimlet-glance, his Japanese or Alexandrian sense of detail; but an endless patience—the patience of the sportsman and the painter—enabled him to track an impression down to its most secret touch. And then he fixed it in one perfect phrase —sometimes just marred by too tense an effort to seize an evanescent reality. Jules Renard, in fine, was an artist.

He looked at Nature, not as so many do, from the fourth floor of a Paris boulevard, but from the village street or from the field that slopes away beyond the orchard hedge. He was mayor of the little commune in the department of the Nièvre where he spent so much of his time—and a mayor passionately absorbed in his municipal affairs; but when he turned homewards and sat down to his writing-table, Chitry-les Mines and Chaumont lost their magic; the man, the mayor, gave place to the patient artist—surely the most scrupulous of our time—carving his cherry-stone, polishing his bead of amber, where some chance insect lives for ever in a pellucid incorruptibility.

This love of detail, this desire to reproduce a landscape, an object or a personage in its individual, intimate truth, are points of contact between Renard and another novelist from the same centre of France : Charles-Louis Philippe. But Philippe's eyes were less keen and his heart was far more tender : Philippe was, as it were, steeped in the Russian pity of a Dostoieffsky. And he knew the poor and the miseries of the poor, not as an artist knows them, mingled with romance, but as the child of poor people who has felt such things at first hand.

He was born in 1874 at Cérilly, a little town of the department of the Allier, where his father was a maker of wooden shoes. A pupil of the board school, his rare abilities promised a prosperous future, and, gifted for mathematics, he studied for the school of engineering—for 'Polytechnique.' But his frail health and tiny size rendered him inapt for that profession, and his livelihood seemed a problem too difficult to solve when Maurice Barrès, a Deputy for Paris, recommended him for a small post in the pay of the town council at the Hôtel-de-Ville. Philippe was thenceforth an inspector of stalls and shop-fronts—and his kind protector chose for him the VII. arondissement of Paris, the Faubourg Saint-Germain, where stalls are few. In return for his nine guineas a month (230 francs) Philippe had but to stroll about the quiet, almost provincial streets of the old-fashioned courtly quarter and reap the harvest of a quiet eye. But Philippe's vision was chiefly interior. In the noble Rue de Varenne and the historical Rue Saint-Dominique he contemplated that abyss of misery, that slippery Avernus of women's lazy wiles and young men's dangerous desire, which he has revealed to us in *Bubu de Montparnasse* and *Marie Donadieu*: tragic idylls of the distant Latin quarter.

Here we seem as far as may be from the pastoral novel! But Philippe, in Paris, saw rise upon his inner eye the Cérilly of his childhood; the one-storied house, opposite his father's shop, where the Père Perdrix lived with his old wife; and the lonely cottage, capped with thatch, where little Charles Blanchard lived alone with his mother, the widowed charwoman, and where the poor, dull, dreamy, ill-nourished lad died at nine years old—of 'old age.' And he saw his own house and his childish self, and his adorable clever mother, and all the poem of their love. And he wrote *Le Père Perdrix*, and *La Mère et l'Enfant*, and he began *Charles Blanchard*. And then, at five-and-thirty years of age, he died.

He cannot be said to have lived in vain, for the young inspector of stalls left behind him, not only a great name to a little clan—a clan which included Barrès, André Gide, Daniel Halévy, Valéry Larbaud, André Beaunier; that is to say, whatever is most delicately critical in France—but also a school. The chief names in that school are Émile Guillaumin and Marguerite Audoux, both of them, like Philippe, natives of the Bourbonnais.

There are, in the literary world of Paris, those who do not scruple to assert that Madame Audoux's great pastoral novel, *Marie-Claire*, was in reality written by Charles-Louis Philippe. I wonder if those inconsiderate critics can have read either author ! It is as though one should accuse Baudelaire of having written the country novels of George Sand; as though one should say that Thomas Hardy really wrote Tennyson's *Idylls of the King*. The incomparable simplicity and serenity of *Marie-Claire* are as different as may be from the difficult harmony, the obscure, subtle, poignant intuitions of Philippe. It is true that Philippe was gaining in simplicity (perhaps from his contact with Madame Audoux?) when he died. And no doubt he was prodigal of counsel, aid, and precept to the little dressmaker who was his pupil in letters : he showed her, perhaps, in a novel, how to 'cut out.' But their genius, their experience, their character, and even their view of life is quite distinct : the one infinitely minute, tormented, tragic; the other large, quiet, and serene; either equally sincere.

It was Madame Audoux who called the friends —the ardent, devoted friends—of Philippe to the nursing home in the Rue de la Chaise, where he lay dying of typhoid fever; it was she, with his mother, summoned from Cérilly, who received his dying breath; and he had often spoken in his circle of the noble imagination, the just and luminous elegance of mind which distinguish *Marie-Claire*. So that when the book appeared there were friends to greet it—the friends of poor Philippe, dead in his grave.

But the book did not need these protectors, for

its success was immediate, popular, immense, and by no means purely literary; readers, who had barely heard of Philippe himself, of André Gide, of any of Madame Audoux's literary clan, opened her volume in their thousands. The story has been translated into several languages—into English, I think. No doubt it owed something to Mirbeau's eloquent preface, revealing the author's personality. The public is sentimental; it was touched by the picture of the poor little dressmaker—not a princess of tape and scissors, but one of those little snips who go out to ladies' houses, working for half a crown a day. The account of this poor woman, no longer quite young, suddenly threatened with blindness if she pursue her trade; turning then, for a consolation, as much as for a means of livelihood, to literature, and with her first venture discovering herself a great artist; this poignant history seemed to the public a novel before the novel began.

Will Marguerite Audoux, intimidated by this rare success, remain the woman of one book? I hope not ! If she dare not again attack the pastoral novel, let her write the touching life of her friend and master, Philippe. Or let her turn from the fields of France to the moving story of a woman alone in Paris, earning the right to live as she draws an interminable thread.

Marie Claire is the history of an orphan girl, brought up in an orphanage, placed out at thirteen years of age as little shepherdess on a farm ; some

five years later—after the merest sketch of a
love-story with her mistress's brother—dismissed;
again received at the orphanage as cook or kitchen-
maid, until, on the last page of all—not yet twenty
years of age, she takes the train for Paris. Can
one imagine anything flatter, staler, more unprofit-
able? Such stories must be written by the thousand
in the simple annals of the poor. And yet *Marie-
Claire* is a sequence of images of unforgettable
loveliness.

The story is divided into three parts; and if the
beginning and the end—the convent and the love-
story—have their rare merits, the middle section,
the life of the little shepherdess on the farm, seems
to me in all sincerity equal to the loveliest pastoral
novels of George Sand—to *François le Champi* or
Le petite Fadette. The shepherdess and her flock
lost in the mist, and that winter scene, when a
'great yellow dog' pounces on a sheep and drags
it away while the collie howls plaintively, crouching
at the shepherdess's feet :—

'Aussitôt je devinai que c'était un loup. Il
emportait le mouton à pleine gueule, par le milieu
du corps. Il grimpa sans effort sur le talus et
quand il sauta le large fossé qui le séparait du bois,
ses pattes de derrière me firent penser à des ailes.
A ce moment je n'aurais pas trouvé extraordinaire
qu'il se fût envolé pardessus les arbres.'

And the personages of the farm : Maître Sylvain,

the kind Pauline, the friendly delicate-minded Eugène, are drawn not only with an artist's sense of beauty, but with a marvellous and mysterious sense of life. In France to-day there are many women writers of great talent and success : Madame Marcelle Tinayre, with her *Maison du Péché*; Madame de Noailles, with her wonderful poems; Mlle Marie Lenéru, with her plays; I admire them all with my heart, but I think I would as soon have written *Marie-Claire* !

Madame Audoux is not the only pupil of Charles-Louis Philippe : Emile Guillaumin is also of his following, or at least he resembles him in his birth-place and his profession. Guillaumin is a farmer who lives on his farm, about ten miles from Cérilly; he works the land with his brother; and, in the intervals of seedtime and harvest he, too, writes pastoral novels about the pleasant country round the Allier river.

But seek not there for the keen, anxious psychology of Philippe, nor for the large poetry of Madame Audoux; nothing could be more matter-of-fact, more *terre-à-terre* (as we say in France), than *La Vie d'un Simple* or *Rose et sa Parisienne*. For that very reason these books, and others from the same pen, are valuable to the inquirer who desires to know, without any alloy of poetry, the real conditions of the farmer's and field-labourer's life in France; but they are not admirable to the artist like the novels of Jules Renard or Marguerite Audoux. Obstinate, precise, Guillaumin delves his style as a peasant tills his land—not (like Philippe or Madame Audoux, who are equally fastidious and minute) in order to produce a certain effect of beauty or impression of sensibility, but in the effort to render a just, exact account of what he has seen.

His best book is *La Vie d'un Simple*. Regarded as art it is dull, monotonous, and bare; and yet, considered as life, it is singularly touching and ample, like one of those vast plains of France, traversed by interminable, poplar-bordered roads, whose great sweeping lines melt, far off, into long, low horizons.

La Vie d'un Simple is the life of a peasant from the time when, a child of seven years old, he pastures his sheep among the stubble and the heather until, an old, bent man, too feeble to work on the land, he again minds the herds at pasture, as they use in France. Tiennou has lived all his life in front of the same horizon; he has no book-learning; he knows nothing but the land; but he knows it well. Like his father before him, he has been a *métayer*, that is to say, a tenant-farmer who combines with the landlord to stock a farm, tills it, and manages the live-stock, and pays his rent on a system of half-profits.

The system is very common in France, and in theory is admirable. It appears a means of uniting capital and labour in the cultivation of the soil. But, if the tenant has no capital behind him, in bad seasons he has to borrow at usurious interest.

And then, if the cart-horse break his neck, or the cow die of anthrax, on the top of a bad harvest, his plight is poor indeed; for the landlord has a right to exact that stock and tools shall always correspond to the inventory drawn up when the tenant entered into possession. And too often, if he improves his farm, the owner makes that an occasion for increasing his own pretensions. Such is the fate of Tiennou, who, having spent the better part of his life on bettering his land, in the end receives notice to quit.

Unless he be (as he so often is) a peasant-proprietor, the lot of the French husbandman is austere. In a little pamphlet, *En Bourbonnais*, M. Guillaumin has added up the yearly receipts of a day-labourer in good work, turn by turn haymaker, harvester, thresher, wood-cutter, and so on. His annual earnings amount, in English coin, to £21 12s. Though he be fed abundantly at the farms where he works all summer long, still his family must live; and he must feed himself all winter-time. And bread is dear in France; out of his twenty guineas a year, the day-labourer must reckon fifteen or sixteen for bread alone. The rent of the cottage will cost another £4; and there remains about 30s. for school expenses, shoes, clothing, fuel, doctoring, wine, tobacco—all the pleasures and luxuries of life. No doubt he sells his pig, and his kids and his poultry, and anything he can, to increase his slender revenues; for, in the valley of the Allier, the peasant is too poor to put a fowl in his pot on Sundays, or enjoy a rasher of his own bacon by his own fireside.

Farther south, among the hills and high valleys of the Cantal, another peasant-farmer, Antonin Dusserre, offers us, in his *Jean et Louise*, another image of pastoral France : the rich yeomanry, the *Couarrous* and *Couarros*, who compose the notable society of those isolated villages, where the château is empty four-fifths of the year or more. The *Couarros* (rich grazing-farmers, intelligent, tenacious, positive, active, and money-loving) compose a rustic middle-class far wealthier than their simple lives would lead us to suppose, proud of their flocks and herds, and their balance at the bankers. M. Dusserre, I believe, is blind; but before that misfortune fell upon him, he has looked long and lovingly at the high-lying heather, the cliffs capped with basalt, the gentian-starred mountain-pastures, and the green glens and *trobers* of his native land. The landscapes and the types of the Cantal live on in his inner eye.

Much farther west, on the borders of Anjou and Vendée, a village schoolmaster, M. Perochon, has recently given us a picture of peasant life in the style of Guillaumin and Dusserre, in *Les Creux-de-Maisons*. A *creux-de-maison* is not, as one might expect, one of those cave-dwellings hewn out of the chalky banks of the Indre or the Loire, which look so primitive but which are said to be dry and cosy, possessing the local reputation of keeping off rheumatism; no, a *creux-de-maison* is a sort of cabin about seven feet high, built of mud or of rough stone cemented with clay, single-roomed, thatch-roofed, with a pane for a window and an earthen floor.

'Cétait une cabane bossue et lépreuse, à peine plus haute qu'un homme; on descendait à l'intéri-eur par deux marches de granit; il y faisait trés sombre, car le jour n'entrait que par une lucarne à deux petits carreaux; l'hiver il y avait de l'eau partout, et cela faisait de la boue qui ne finissait de sècher, sous les lits surtout; il y avait des trous qui empêchaient les tabourets de tenir debout; on les bouchait de temps en temps avec de la terre apportée du jardin.'

Such are the *creux-de-maisons*, still not infrequent round Bressuire in Vendée, though happily rarer every year, as the spread of creameries and co-operatives brings the sense and the means of comfort into the Ireland of France. M. Pérochon is perhaps a little unfair in taking no notice of this clearing of the horizon : he will not allow us a gleam of consolation ; Zola himself was never more resolutely lugubrious. His book is con-ceived in a low tone, a minor key, by a deliberate purpose, and we must accept the artist's postulate.

His theme is the life of a day-labourer from the day he leaves the regiment till the time when, at forty-eight years of age, having buried wife

and child, he owns that life has been too much
for him. He has had his romance, has married
the miller's lovely daughter, and has seen her
die of want in the horrible *creux-de-maison*. He
has watched the children grow thinner month by
month.

'Depuis le Mardi-Gras, mes pauvres petits n'ont
mangé ni lard, ni œufs, ni lait . . . quatre livres
de beurre en tout depuis quatre mois. . . . Je
suis fatiguée de n'avoir rien à faire manger aux
petits; des haricots et des pommes de terre, des
pommes de terre et des haricots! Pas moyen
seulement d'élever des poules!'

And indeed in the poorer parts of frugal France,
so royally fertile, there are many districts where
the married labourer in winter used to have little
more in his larder; where a sack of potatoes, a
sack of chestnuts, and a sack of buck-wheat
supplied the chief of his diet, or at least of his
children's diet if he be fed at the farm. I speak
in the past tense, but I fear it is so to-day in many
a village of Lozère or Brittany, where the food of
the agricultural poor is as much worse than it is
in England, as it is better and more varied in
Normandy or Anjou or Touraine. And this
constant strife between hunger and love, between
natures naturally tender, gay, and brave, and
circumstances continually depressing—has resulted
in a stampede towards the towns, a rural exodus,

which is the great problem of the day in the poorer provinces of France.

The war has singularly respected the writers of Pastoral novels. It has even added to their ranks a new name, that of M. Henri Bachelin, whose village tales, *Le Serviteur*, in 1918, *Le Village*, in 1919, are direct and living sketches of rural France in the minute and finely-stippled taste of Emile Guillaumin.

THE NOVEL OF CHILDHOOD

EDMOND JALOUX, ANDRÉ LAFON, G. DES VOISINS,
MARCEL PROUST, ETC.

Two of the pastoral novels we have just considered, *Charles Blanchard* and *Marie-Claire*, are novels of childhood; and the first two volumes (the most beautiful) of *Jean-Christophe* come into the same category; when we examined the works of René Boylesve, we found that the hero of two of his most touching stories is a little boy; Anatole France is even now writing the history of 'Petit Pierre'; Francis Jammes has consecrated a whole volume to the observation of his baby daughter; and there is Mæterlinck's exquisite *Oiseau Bleu*. And here are several other writers who, in the last half-dozen years, have written novels of conspicuous beauty and reputation concerned with little children.

When I came to live in France, some thirty years ago, the novel of childhood was supposed to be a product of English manufacture, almost exclusively. It was much admired, for the French are a nation of child-lovers and a people of psychologists; but it was generally supposed that Anglo-Saxon blood was needed to relate the youth of a Maggie Tulliver or a David Copperfield. In those days the French yellowback, in six cases out of ten, was a love story; in the other four it was a social novel.

Is it the philosophy of Bergson, his glorification of instinct, sensibility, intuition, that has changed all that? The novel of childhood is now one of the most frequent, the most admired of French romances. Not the mere observation of childhood; not the sole charm of reminiscence, always popular because it aureoles our faded foreheads with the light of other days: 'Ah! so I used to think! Even so was I!' It is rather a careful reconstruction of the point of view of a young boy—except Marie-Claire, I remember no girls in the novel of childhood!—and his first impressions of the mysteries of life: love, sin, pain, madness, death. These novels of childhood are, in fact, studies in psychology.

Dickens perhaps began it—Dickens always so beloved in France. Yet Oliver Twist, David Copperfield, Little Nell, if they suffer from the world's oppression, suffer rather than reflect or observe. The theme was really inaugurated, I think, by Mr Henry James, some fifteen years ago, in *What Maisie Knew*, the impression made on a child by the mysterious iniquity of its elders.

M. René Boylesve was the first: *L'Enfant à la Balustrade* appeared, if I remember right, in 1903. We have considered in another chapter the provincial studies of this exquisite author; here I will only draw attention to his childish hero. Riquet Nadaud, the narrator of *La Becquée* and

L'Enfant à la Balustrade,[1] is a little boy who has
been sent, on the death of his mother, to live with
his maternal grandparents in their old-fashioned
house in the country near La Haye-Descartes.
How charming his descriptions of the child's
walks in the fields with brusque and capable Tante
Félicie I have had occasion to declare elsewhere.
For the moment my concern is with little Nadaud
when, after his father's re-marriage, he goes back
to live with his parents at Loches.

The stepmother is a gentle, languid, gracious
creature, born in America though French by race,
a beautiful Creole from Louisiana. Needless to
say, she is bored to death at Loches—not quite at
first, when her young loveliness, her position as
bride, her gift for music, ensure her a certain
social importance and consideration. But her
husband, the notary, cribbed and confined in his
narrow house—mindful, too, that his first wife's
death had been in some degree attributed to that
house's sunlessness—secures the reversion of the
handsomest building in the town, after the actual
owner's death. Unfortunately, M. Nadaud was
not the only man who had set his heart on that
comely residence ! Soon the town is up in arms
against the lawyer for stealing his march on others,
and poor Tantine, the foreign wife, is left alone
in her dull parlour with Riquet for her sole society.

Riquet—and young Dr Troufleau, faithful to

[1] Translated into English under the title of *The House on
the Hill.* David Watt, 1904.

his friends. Excellent Troufleau, awkwardest, honestest of men! Charming Tantine, without an evil thought in her feather-head! Alas, opportunity, thy guilt is great! Out of sheer boredom on her part and simple pity on his, they are drawn quite close to the edge of the abyss—close enough to feel its attraction, its dizzy, strange, reluctant fascination—under the sensitive eyes of the child who knows nothing of passion or of sin. Doubtless that innocent presence it is that saves them; they recoil in time.

M. Nadaud at last realises that his wife is being enervated by solitude, demoralised by idleness, deprived of energy to resist the simplest temptations. She needs social intercourse. A few visitors, a little appreciation of her music and her beauty, and Troufleau would soon occupy his proper place in her regard—that of a kind, friendly young man, smothered in an absurd frock-coat and honestly in love with another woman.

So the husband puts his pride in his pocket, and reconciles himself with his neighbours; and things soon right themselves. Only a child has apprehended that which does not belong to the world of a child, only a boy's lofty pure-minded ideal has been injured by contact with the hard realities of life.

Madame Tinayre, in a volume of stories, L'Amour Pleure (1908), took up the tale a few years later. Robert Marie is a lad of fifteen, sixteen, seventeen, regarded as a ward by the notary of Beaugency and his wife, Uncle Bon and Aunt Belle. He has no relations, only his godfather and godmother, M. and Mme Cheverny, who live in Paris, and who from time to time come down to see him. Robert can remember a time, long distant, when there was no uncle Bon, no Aunt Belle, but, so far back as his mind can carry, there have always been a M. and Mme Cheverny, and always they have come to see him together.

He knows there is a mystery about his real parents; and the different suppositions he makes concerning them, the gradual growth of his desire to know who he really is, are the substance of this haunting story; but not for a moment does he suppose that M. and Mme Cheverny (who seem the sole links between him, poor waif, and those other boys who have a place in the world, parents, a name) are not really M. and Mme Cheverny, are not married : they whom he has not ever seen apart !—are each of them married to another. And he is their son, brought up by stealth, visited in mystery. The contrast between the passion of these unhappy, charming parents and the robust indignant innocence of their unconscious son is told with a sincerity and a romantic realism peculiar, I think, to the work of Madame Tinayre.

About the same time—a year later, I think—in 1909, a young writer from Marseilles, M. Edmond Jaloux, published his *Le Reste est Silence*, which obtained the Prix Vie Heureuse for that year. There are many points of contact between this novel and *L'Enfant à la Balustrade*; but M. Jaloux has not the more than feminine delicacy, the subtle moral tenderness of M. Boylesve. He, too, tells the story of a small boy, the surprised, half-unconscious involuntary witness of the growth of an unlawful love. Madame Meisserel is a less innocent, less charming Tantine, and here, too, there is a dull, awkward, not unpathetic husband.

The delicate sky, the gracious landscape of Touraine are replaced by the busy brilliance of Marseilles; the key is higher, the sonority is louder; and it is well that this is so; we need a dose of southern brutality—or at least callousness—to enable us to digest the supposition that it is the son of Madame Meisserel (now grown up) who revives in reminiscence the history of his dead mother's guilty passion, as he witnessed it in his seventh year. How wise was M. Boylesve to make his little boy a stepson, and the charming step-mother almost innocent—a little frivolous at worst. We suspect Madame Meisserel of having gone to greater lengths and yet we scarce forgive her son his tone of superiority.

The same theme, in 1912, furnished M. Gilbert des Voisins with the matter of *L'Enfant qui prit Peur*. Here the plot is pushed to a tragedy; the child, aghast to find the serpent rampant in his little Eden, and his father's friend his mother's lover, commits suicide. We are still further here from M. Boylesve's exquisite moral delicacy.

We neighbour it again in *L'Elève Gilles*, the first novel of a young schoolmaster which, in

1912, obtained the new great prize of the French Academy—the prize of £400, as yet only twice bestowed : once on *Jean-Christophe* and once on the too-slender but charming book before us. (I mention all these prizes to show the undoubted popularity of the theme, and may add that M. des Voisins' book very nearly obtained a Prix Vie Heureuse.)

Gilles is a little boy suddenly sent from home to live with an old aunt in the country because his father is suffering from neurasthenia and needs a complete rest : no noise, no movement about him. The child's mother takes him and leaves him with her aunt and the old servant, Segonde, whose portrait is one of the charms of the volume; and though the lad is happy enough with them, we feel there is something poignant behind—something we do not know, and that the child does not even suspect. He is sent to the grammar school of the little town near his aunt's property, and we feel that the shadow—the unsuspected shadow— hangs over him, there, too, increasingly evident to those about him, though still invisible to the child narrator.

Little by little, by a word here, a silence there, by the sensitive temperament of the child himself, by the strangeness of the father (who has come for rest and change to the quiet country house) we learn the truth : the man is mad. Gilles never knows it; but if he is so quiet, so sensitive, and so solitary, it is because the whole little world around him marks him for the madman's child; a being to be spared, respected, but not played with like another boy. He is a child apart.

No chapter in my book has a more delightful choice of reading than is offered by these Novels of Childhood. And among the most enchanting of all I would place *Le Grand Meaulnes.* Henri Alain-Fournier leapt into being (from a literary point of view) in 1913 with this strange romantic little novel. The book is not of our time in the least, though without any affectation of archaism. It appears related far more nearly to George Sand's *Petite Fadette,* or to some tale of Musset's, or to Gérard de Nerval's *Sylvie,* than to any Twentieth Century production; and I think the closest we can get to it in our own times would be one of the more poetical of Hardy's Wessex novels, before he fell into the tragic pessimism of *Tess* or *Jude.* The poetry, the fantasy, is all in the author's imagination; for what, I ask you, could be less romantic than the setting of his tale—a Training College for Primary Education, or rather a large village Board-School, with a class reserved for future teachers,—even though it be situate in the very heart of Berry? And yet over every page of *Le Grand Meaulnes* there slips and trembles the light that never was on sea or land. The heroes are two lads of fifteen and seventeen; and rarely has any author rendered more delicately the prestige of the big boy for the little boy, and the chivalrous half-mystic hero-worship in which he walks enveloped. The mystery, the beauty, the wonderfulness of the poet's world transfigure the homely story, which is merely that of a school-boy of fifteen who runs away from school, who misses his way and gets caught up in the whirl of a large country wedding at a quaint half-ruined manor-house whose name he does not know. Never again can the lad find that manor or that beautiful girl who was the bridegroom's sister, with whom he has fallen in love. And at last his boy friend, 'le grand Meaulnes' discovers her, but keeps her for himself; the capricious, fascinating Meaulnes marries that fairy Princess and deserts her on the morrow, leaving her for all companion-ship and consolation the adoring devotion of the humble friend, who tells the story.

Those first rays of fame, which are brighter than the rising sun, slipped over the young author's fresh horizon. And then the war broke out. Henri Alain-Fournier set out for Lorraine, a Lieutenant in the Reserve; on September 22, 1914, he was reported missing. For many months, for nearly a year, the hope that dazzles so many tearful eyes —the hope that he was retained by the Germans a prisoner in the invaded provinces, from which no communication was allowed with France—sustained his family and friends and that portion of the public who, like myself, watched his career with sympathy. And then, one day last summer, I heard the sad story.

A young lieutenant, fresh from the Polytechnique, the son of one of my friends, fell in with Alain-

Fournier during those months of victory and retreat on the frontier of Lorraine. The two young men, no less ardent in their intellectual energy than in their military theories, recognised each other as kindred spirits; with a third (a young pastor, I think, or the son of a Protestant pastor) they used to meet o' nights, their day's work done, in a broken-down military motor car, wrecked by the side of the road. I like to think of the three young officers, on those August nights—the immense French camp asleep all round them—as they sat till the dawn broke, like gipsies in their van, eagerly talking *de omni re scibili*. In the daytime they generally saw little of each other; but, on August 22, one of the two others, marching to the front, met Alain-Fournier and his men going in a contrary direction. 'Ordered to the rear! (he called out); no luck! Au revoir!'; and he passed on. It chanced that that day's engagement was a particularly murderous one, but the two friends when they met at night felt no anxiety about the third of their accustomed party, deeming him safe. And yet, when the dead were counted and buried, there was one figure, the head bashed in, whose limbs and hands bore so great a resemblance to their friend that the young men felt a chill presentiment. They looked for the badge of identity; a wicked bayonet-thrust had driven it into the breast. So haunting was their surmise that they cut it out; but they could not decipher the number on the battered, bloodstained plaque.

Since then, unbroken silence : Alain-Fournier is among the 'missing.'

Of all these books—save, perhaps, Alain-Fournier's, for which I have, I own, a peculiar weakness; of all these novels of childhood—unless I except M. Boylesve's, and *Marie-Claire*, and *Jean-Christophe* (for so many of them, when you come to think of it, are really quite first-rate)—the most delicate, the most pregnant with a sensibility extraordinarily rich, and ample, and yet sensitive as the impressions of convalescence or the first images of childhood, is an immense novel, published in the winter of 1913-14 by M. Marcel Proust, under the enigmatic title, *A la Recherche du Temps Perdu : Du Côté de chez Swann*. The book with which it is easiest to compare it, is Henry James's *A Small Boy*, though that, indeed, is concise and simple compared with M. Marcel Proust's attempt at reconstituting the vague shimmering impressions of a young mind, the wonderment with which—inexplicably to us—it regards places and people which in our eyes possess no magic. M. Proust's hero is a small boy living in the bosom of the most regular of families—one of those vast French families, closely knit, whose tissue unites grandparents, great-aunts, uncles, cousins in such quantity as to limit the possible supply of outside acquaintance. One most familiar friend, however, there is, the friend of the family, a 'hereditary friend,' as Homer would say, M. Swann. He is a man of the world, a member of the Jockey Club, a friend of

the Prince of Wales, a comrade of the Comte de
Paris, a great collector; but for the small boy and
his family he is especially 'le fils Swann,' the son
of their old friend the member of the Stock Exchange
('qui a bien dû lui laisser quatre ou cinq millions') who
has made a ridiculous marriage with a demi-mondaine
—a case of all for love and the world well lost.

And the world is lost the more completely that
the impossible lady continues her adventures
unabashed and unabated after matrimony. She
therefore is not 'received,' or indeed hardly men-
tioned, in the ample respectable home of the small
boy; so that Swann and this unlikely love of
Swann's, this beautiful wife of Swann's, and Swann's
remote, intangible, but not invisible little girl, are
the constant objects of his romantic curiosity.

There are two walks at Combray : you may
set out in the direction of Guermantes or else go
round by Swann's : 'du côté de chez Swann,' and
to the childish hero of the book these two walks
gradually accumulate round them the material for
two views of life—Swann standing for all that is
brilliant, irregular, attractive, Guermantes representing an orderly and glorious tradition. This
long novel, *A la Recherche du Temps Perdu*, sets
out to recover, in three volumes, a child's first
impressions in both sorts; but this instalment
records (in 500 closely printed pages) the earliest
images '*du côté de chez Swann* : images forgotten by
the intellect, mysteriously resuscitated by the
senses—by a tune sung in the street, or a whiff of

thyme or mignonette, or (as in the case of our author) by the flavour of a fragment of sponge-cake dipped in tea; images in which matter and memory are subtly combined in a sudden warm flood of life, revived, without the intervention of the understanding.

In all this the influence of Bergson is evident. But can we imagine the Twentieth Century in France without Bergson? As well conceive the Eighteenth Century without Rousseau. Such a delicate excess of sensibility does not exist without disorder; such a need to fuse and unite the very depth of the soul with the ambient world—such a sense of the fluid, pregnant, moving flood of life—exceeds the strict limits of a perfect art. Evidently M. Proust's novel, by its faults as well as by its qualities, is admirably adequate to the spirit of our age. Again, I repeat that, while I read with delight the delicate, long-winded masters of our times, I think sometimes with regret of a Turgeneff, no less subtle, who, even as they, wrote at tremendous length and recorded the minutest shades of feeling, but, having finished, went through his manuscript again, pen in hand, and reduced it to about one-third of its original length.

In the case of M. Proust's novel, the result is the more bewildering that the book is conceived, as it were, on two planes; no sooner have we accustomed ourselves to the sun-pierced mist of early reminiscence than the light changes; we find ourselves in glaring noon; the recollection becomes a recital; the magic glory fades from M. Swann and the fair, frail Odette de Crécy; we see them in their habit as they lived and moved among their acquaintance; we smile at the evocation of an artistic coterie under President Grévy, and suffer a sort of gnawing under our ribs as we realise the poignant jealousy of the unhappy Swann. And then the light shifts again; we are back in childhood; and Swann is again the mysterious idol of a dreamy, chivalrous little boy :—

'Il me semblait un être si extraordinaire que je trouvais merveilleux que des personnes que je fréquentais le connussent aussi et que dans les hasards d'une journée quelconque on peutêtre amené à le rencontrer. Et une fois ma mère, en train de nous raconter comme chaque soir, à diner, les courses qu'elle avait faites dans l'après-midi, rien qu'en disant : " A ce propos, devinez qui j'ai rencontre aux Trois Quartiers, au rayon des parapluies : Swann," fit éclore au milieu de son récit, fort aride pour moi, une fleur mysterieuse. Quelle mélancolique volupté d'apprendre que cet après-midi-là, profilant dans la foule sa forme surnaturelle, Swann avait été acheter un parapluie.'

Can I end better than with this brief and casual quotation, which, better than my criticism, will show the fresh and fine reality which these pages mysteriously recover from the back of our consciousness (where it exists in a warm penumbra of its own) and exhale, as naturally as vapour from a new-ploughed autumn furrow? Something older and deeper than knowledge pervades the book.

EPILOGUE

As we glance from across the Channel at these writers, so often consciously opposed, the charm of distance blends the tints, harmonises the outlines, and shows us in most of them a certain similarity. They are children of Dionysos, not of Apollo; they are mystics, not materialists; they conceive existence as a great religious symphony which you must experience and not seek to understand. More than once, in reading the most liberal and modern among them, the words of the Catholic, Claudel, have risen to my lips :—

'Il ne faut pas comprendre; il faut perdre connaissance !'

They have, most of them, the intuition of a state transcending reality—I mean objective reality. Yet, notwithstanding this spiritual ideal, they set a high value on action, on social energy. I have just said that, as a rule the French writers of the Twentieth Century are mystics, but they are not ecstatics wrapt in a solitary trance; they are eager to act on men and women, to bind them in associations—though, of course, their groups are different, for some of them are Socialists, like our pastoral novelists; many are Nationalists from points of view as different as Rostand and Boylesve and Barrès; and to some the only vital bond is a religion (since they are French, naturally the Roman Catholic religion).

They are almost all Intuitionalists; and, in almost all of them there is the same reaction from the Individualism of the Nineteenth Century. The influence of Bergson is evident, and also that of the Symbolists of the closing Nineteenth Century. They are anti-rationalists, almost to a man—or a woman; for it is perhaps symptomatic that the feminine writers should be so abundant and so remarkable in the younger generation.

There is something primitive, elementary, spontaneous, romantic, in much of their art which will often remind the middle-aged English reader of our pre-Raphaelites of yesterday, but which is, really, even more akin to the modern Irish revival, on the one hand, and to the school of Dostoieffsky in Russia. Although they are as national as they are nationalist, these symbolists and mystics do not seem to us English easily recognisable as French, because we do not remember that France is Celtic as well as Latin, sentimental no less than witty, a land of saints as well as a land of pleasant sinners; and that Pascal and Fénelon, Vincent de Paul and Joan of Arc, are no less characteristic of France than are Montaigne or Voltaire.